Reconciled

Brandon Vaughan

WestBow
P R E S S
A DIVISION OF THOMAS NELSON

WestBow Press books may be ordered through booksellers or by contacting:

WestBow Press
A Division of Thomas Nelson
1663 Liberty Drive
Bloomington, IN 47403
www.westbowpress.com
1-(866) 928-1240

ISBN: 978-1-4497-8526-0 (sc)
ISBN: 978-1-4497-8525-3 (e)
ISBN: 978-1-4497-8532-1 (hc)
Library of Congress Control Number: 2013902753

Scripture taken from the King James Version of the Bible.

Printed in the United States of America
WestBow Press rev. date: 2/18/2013

Dedication

THIS BOOK IS DEDICATED IN MEMORY of Brother Ernie Perham. There was never a better teacher on the home and family, neither in sermon nor example. His Godly wisdom was and still is a beacon to countless families around the world. Everyone that's had the privilege of meeting him and his family has been touched in one way or another. His ministry now lives on through the lives of his wife and children, and I have no doubt that he's very proud of the young men and women that they have become. He was never too busy to give a concerned ear to this young preacher. Even after he left us, his advice gave me direction in my darkest hour, and I am forever grateful. I look forward to the day when I can thank him in person.

For if, when we were enemies, we were reconciled to God by the death of his Son, much more, being reconciled, we shall be saved by his life.

—Romans 5:10

Contents

Appendixes:

Introduction

When a Trial Becomes a Trophy

IT IS NO SECRET TO CHRISTIANS that they serve an all-powerful God. His mighty, sovereign hand is ever present in our lives, working all things to the good of those who love Him and are called according to His purpose. There is no doubt that some of His provisions and miracles go unnoticed in our everyday lives. But every now and then the Lord does something so amazing, so spectacular, that even nonbelievers can't help but be touched in one way or another.

Whenever I think about this truth, my mind goes back to the ageless story of David and Goliath. Standing at nine feet, nine inches tall, Goliath was an intimidating force. This captain of the Philistines stood before the armies of Israel, daring any man to challenge him. For forty days he declared that, if any man from Israel would fight and defeat him, the Philistines would be Israel's servants. However, no one, not even King Saul, dared to fight him.

Then along came this young shepherd boy by the name of David. The only reason he was at the battlefield was because his father had sent him to bring food to his brothers. Not long after David arrived on the scene, Goliath went before the armies of Israel with his same insults and his challenge. David was enraged. He said, "Who is this uncircumcised Philistine, that he should defy the armies of the living God?"

After much convincing, King Saul agreed to let this youth fight to the death with this giant. David knew that the Lord would win the battle for him. Armed only with a small staff, a sling, and five smooth stones he had taken from a brook, David went out to fight this great man of war.

As David approached Goliath, he shouted to him, "This day will the Lord deliver thee into mine hand." As the giant ran to him, David placed a stone into his sling and let it fly. The stone sunk into Goliath's forehead, and down he went. The Lord had won the battle for David and for Israel.

Think about the scene of this young shepherd boy slinging a stone at that giant and his body falling to the earth. I bet that, for those first few moments after Goliath hit the ground, such a holy hush fell over that place that you could've heard a pin drop. There stood both the people of God and the enemies of God, watching as this miracle took place. No one of a sane mind could have given David credit for what happened that day. After all, Goliath's sword was almost as big as David! No doubt, people went home that day talking not so much about what David had done but rather about what God had done.

Through David, the Lord had turned a trial into a great trophy. What was once, "We can never defeat that great and terrible giant of war," turned into, "God delivered us from the hands of Goliath and the Philistines with just a shepherd boy and a sling!"

The Lord has brought one of those "holy hush" events into our lives, and my mother and I feel compelled to tell it. We want to share our "trophy" with the world. And we are confident that the readers will know that God did it.

We're not seeking to evoke temporary, emotional feelings. Rather, we want others to make life-changing decisions as a result of what the Lord has done in our lives. We want to see lost souls come to a saving knowledge of Jesus Christ. We want Christians to be comforted and strengthened as they wait for the Lord to turn their trials into trophies. And we want the young girl out there who is pregnant and scared because she has no means to care for a child to know that there is hope! If there is one thing that we have learned through this experience, it is that God has a plan for every life, and that no one is here by accident. Dear reader, your life is precious to God. He gave His only begotten Son, Jesus Christ, that you might have life and have it more abundantly. Lost person, will you give your soul to Him? Christian will you give your life to Him?

The great evangelist D. L. Moody once said, "The world has yet to see what God can do with a man fully consecrated to him. By God's help, I aim to be that man." Could you be that man or that woman who stands in the gap for someone else? How might God use your life to help others in need? Consider these things as you read this book. We hope it will be a blessing to you.

1

A Bombshell: Cheryl's Story

But if ye will not do so, behold, ye have sinned against the LORD: and be sure your sin will find you out.
—Numbers 32:23

THERE ARE MOMENTS IN THE LIFE of every person, unexpected moments, that drop in and change everything. These bombshell moments can come in the form of a tragic death in the family, a spouse confessing an affair, a grim report from the doctor, or a violent storm that destroys everything one has ever worked for in a matter of seconds. People can remember every detail about where they were and what they were doing when such bombshells were dropped into their lives. My bombshell came in the form of a child. I know that sounds cruel, but the truth is that for a nineteen-year-old girl with no support and no direction in life, pregnancy was the worst possible news.

I will never forget that day at the doctor's office. It was a humid Florida day in the spring of 1984. For weeks I had experienced just about all of the textbook signs of pregnancy, but I *had* to make sure. Maybe I was just sick. Perhaps I was irregular. Could it be that I was just paranoid? I desperately hoped that the doctor would denounce my suspicions and send me on my way.

I drove to the family clinic not far from where I lived in the small town of Winter Haven, Florida. I didn't tell a soul about my appointment—or even about my suspicions for that matter. I sat down and filled out the paperwork, as is the usual custom. I then handed it to the nurse and again took my seat.

The waiting room was so crowded that day, I almost felt claustrophobic. The whole world seemed like it was closing in on me. My eyes began to scan the room for people I knew, and thankfully, there weren't any. I don't know how long I waited; it seemed like an eternity. Finally a nurse stepped out and said with a loud voice, "Cheryl Heath." I quickly followed her down the hallway and into a small examination room. She handed me a gown and said, "The doctor will be in shortly," and out she went.

I changed into the gown and sat down on the examination table. I sat there for a few minutes, listening to all the typical sounds of a busy doctor's office: people talking, children crying, phones ringing, footsteps walking up and down the hall. The rooms were separated by curtains instead of walls, so it was a little nerve-racking, to say the least. I felt so alone, and as I sat there my mind began to race. I couldn't help but think to myself, *How did it get to this point?*

I began to reflect on my life as a young girl growing up in central Florida. I was the youngest of four children and the only girl. My father had walked out on us when I was just a year old, never again to come into our lives. My mom had tried her best as a single mother to make ends meet, but as you can imagine, life was pretty tough. When I was eight, my mother remarried. But this change proved only to take us out of the frying pan and into the fire. My step-dad was a tyrant and an alcoholic. My older brothers David and Rick had already moved out by this time. But my brother Doug and I were stuck witnessing the drinking, partying, and violence that come with alcoholism. He was pretty much the only father I ever knew, and my mother was with him until I was about eighteen and they divorced.

Despite my home life, I was always a pretty good kid. I made good grades and stayed out of trouble—that is, until I turned seventeen. It all started one day after school. My friend Stacy came over to the house to hang out for a while. We had the whole house to ourselves. Everyone else was out doing their own thing. We were sitting on the back porch talking when Stacy pulled something out of her pocket. She held it up and said, "Cheryl, do you know what this is?"

"I think so," I replied.

"Come on. Take a hit with me," Stacy said.

Deep down, I knew it wasn't right. But then again, why not? It was my life, and it was about time that I lived it. At least that's what I told myself.

There I was, smoking weed on my back porch with Stacy. I had never so much as taken a puff of a cigarette or tasted a beer. Sure, I had some guilt and some reservations, but they were all drowned out by this new liberty I had found. This was the turning point in my life that led me down a spiraling road of partying, sex, and alcohol.

Within two years I had gone from a quiet, shy, Goody Two-shoes to an out-and-out rebel. My grades dropped so badly that I almost didn't graduate from high school. And now, here I sat in the doctor's office at age nineteen, secretly getting a pregnancy test. I couldn't blame my parents—or anyone else for that matter. I had made my own choices and deserved whatever I got. But what if I *was* pregnant? What about the child? It was totally innocent. Well maybe, just maybe, I wasn't pregnant.

All of a sudden I was jolted out of my thoughts by the curtain being jerked aside. Much to my dismay, it was the familiar face of Doctor Perry. It wasn't that he was a bad guy. It was just that he knew my mom, and I was afraid he might snitch. I could tell that he was a little surprised to see me there for a pregnancy test, but he did his best to be professional. "Hi, Cheryl," he said. "It's good to see you. Lie back on the table, and I'll begin the examination."

As he began the examination, I could feel all of my nerves start to kick in. This was the moment of truth. I knew that any second he was going to say those three dreaded words: "Yep, you're pregnant." But much to my surprise, he told me to get dressed and that he would be back in a minute. That was all he said as he darted out of the room.

As I changed into my clothes, I couldn't help but wonder what was going on. Was something seriously wrong with me? Was I pregnant? *Oh no*, I thought to myself. *He's going to call Mom and tell her first!* I was beginning to feel a pit in my stomach.

Finally, he ripped back the curtain once again, and I'll never forget what he said: "Yep, you're pregnant, but you probably already knew that. So, is this good news?" I could sense the sarcasm in his voice. I was too shaken to answer. I just sat there in shock. It took every ounce of determination in me not to burst into tears. The doctor, seeing my reaction, said, "I'll have the nurse sign you out." And he disappeared down the hallway.

I made my way out to the car. I sat down in the driver's seat and closed the door behind me. I just sat there and wept for the longest time. I couldn't believe this was actually happening! A bombshell had fallen hard, and life as I knew it would never be the same.

What was I going to do? So many questions began to fill my mind. What was I going to do with the baby? Should I tell the father? Oh no! How was I going to explain this to Mom?

2
Coming Clean

He that covereth his sins shall not prosper:
but whoso confesseth and forsaketh them shall have
mercy.
—Proverbs 28:13

WHEN I FINALLY MANAGED TO REGAIN some measure of composure, I began the drive home. I was absolutely terrified of what awaited me when I got there. That drive home felt as if I was walking the "Green Mile." I just knew that Dr. Perry had called Mother and told her all about my visit.

After what seemed like a matter of seconds, I pulled into my driveway. Mom's car was there, so I knew she was home. *Here it goes*, I thought to myself. *Time to face the music.* I slowly got out of the car and walked to the front door. I could feel my heart pounding in my chest; my legs began to feel like Jell-O as I got closer to the house. I grabbed the doorknob, took a deep breath, and walked inside.

As I made my way through the living room and down the hall, I could see that Mom's bedroom door was closed. I tiptoed up to her door and listened in. I could hear her stirring around like she was getting ready to go somewhere. I didn't want to intrude on her, so I sat down on the couch and turned on the television, waiting for the wrath to come. Maybe I could find something to occupy my mind, but it wasn't likely. I hadn't been there but a few minutes when I heard her bedroom door open. "Here we go," I said under my breath.

My mother walked into the room, and much to my surprise, she said, "Hey, Cheryl, how was your day?"

How was my day? Was she *kidding*? Was she giving me an opportunity to come clean, or could it be that the doctor really *hadn't* called her? As quickly and calmly as I could get the words out, I said, "It was okay, nothing special."

"Well all right, then," she said. "I'm going to town, so make sure to lock the door behind me."

"Yes, ma'am," I said in disbelief. She had no idea! She was clueless!

Now I knew that the mature thing to do would be to sit her down right then and just lay it all out for her. But hey, why ruin her night out on the town? I can't tell you the relief I felt when she walked out of the house that evening. But I knew that the victory would be short-lived. After all, it's not like you can hide the fact that you're carrying a human being around inside of you. I would tell her. It just wasn't going to be that night.

Well the days turned into weeks, and the weeks turned into a month, and I still hadn't gathered up the courage to tell her. I hadn't told a soul for that matter. I knew that my time was running out. I was now four months pregnant, and I *had* to take action. It was clear to me by this time that I couldn't face Mom alone; I needed support. However, my options were limited. My brothers Rick and Doug were off doing their own thing at the time. I didn't have any close friends, and the baby's father wasn't in the picture. We hadn't been together that long, and we had broken it off not long before I found out that I was pregnant. He might have stuck by me and done the right thing, but I couldn't take that chance. The last thing I needed was for someone to try and pressure me into getting an abortion. Then it hit me. Of course! I could tell my brother David.

David was a good bit older than me. At that point, he had moved out and been married for some time. David and his wife Debbie are some of the most kindhearted people I know. They would listen, and they would support me.

After a few minutes of psyching myself up, I picked up the phone and called David. The phone rang a couple of times, and then I heard the gentle voice of my brother on the other end. "Hello."

"Hey, David, it's Cheryl," I said in a meek tone.

"Hey, Cheryl, how are you doing? I haven't heard from you in a while."

"I'm doing okay," I replied. I wasn't in a mood for small talk, so I cut right to the chase. "Look, David, I know this is kind of out-of-the-blue, but I really need to sit down and talk to you about something."

Without hesitation, David replied, "Sure, I'll be home all evening."

I told him I would be there in an hour, and we hung up. As I began to get ready, I could already feel a lump in my throat. There wasn't going to be anything easy about this, and that was clear to me.

As I pulled into David's driveway, I could once again feel my nerves raging. They seemed to come on like clockwork. But there was no turning back this time. The truth *had* to come out.

I walked up the sidewalk to the front porch. Before I could even knock on the door, David was there to welcome me in. "Hey, sis," he said with a smile. "Come on in and have a seat." He gave me a big hug as I walked in the door. It was a very reassuring gesture.

As we sat down, his wife Debbie walked in from the kitchen. "Hello, Cheryl! It's so nice to see you," she said in her usual welcoming tone.

"Good to see you too," I said with as much enthusiasm as I could muster.

"Would you like something to drink," she asked.

"No, thank you."

Then she asked the question that I knew she was pondering: "Would you like me to give you two some privacy?"

"No, you can stay here with us. It's fine with me." I knew that it would soon be common knowledge anyway. What could it hurt? So she took a seat next to David on the love seat.

David broke the silence almost immediately. "So, what's on your mind, Cheryl?"

"David, I need your help." I could already feel tears beginning to well up in my eyes. *Come on, Cheryl, hold it together,* I thought to myself. "I'm … I'm … David, I'm pregnant, and I need you to be with me when I tell Mom." The tears were flowing uncontrollably now. I just put my head in my hands and waited for a response. They paused for a moment in obvious shock.

Then David calmly said, "Cheryl, everything's going to be all right. We'll go with you to talk to Mom, and everything will work out." Even though his answer seemed rather cliché, I was so thankful and relieved that they had agreed to go with me.

I calmed down after a few minutes. We sat and talked for a while about some of the details of the pregnancy. And then David asked me a question that completely caught me off guard: "So, are you planning on keeping the baby?"

Wow, what a thought. There was a child coming in about five months, and what was I going to do with it? I started to cry again as I began to answer his question. "In a perfect world, of course I would love to keep my baby." But of course, it *wasn't* a perfect world—far from it, as a matter of fact. Could I raise a child? *Should* I? Could I really be a good mother and provide a nurturing environment? I began to lose control of my emotions as I pondered these questions. Deep down, I knew the answer to those questions was a resounding *no*.

David and Debbie once again tried to console me, and after a while I settled down. They could see that talking about it was tearing me up, so they changed the subject. We continued with some small talk for a little while, and just before I left, we all agreed to meet at my house the following evening in order to break the news to Mom. We hugged and said our goodbyes, and I went on my way.

I lay there in my bed that night with everything but sleep on my mind. I couldn't help but think what Mom's reaction would be. I realized that I was at her mercy, and I didn't deserve it. I knew that she wouldn't condone what I had done, and rightfully so. But if she would at least be supportive, then maybe, just maybe, I could keep the baby and at least try to give it a good home. Without her support, there was seemingly no way that I could keep and care for a baby. Mom's decision would no doubt change the course of my life one way or another. I was emotionally exhausted, and at some point during the night, my thoughts gave way to a deep sleep.

Judgment day finally came, and despite my efforts to keep busy, the day just seemed to drag on and on. I must have looked at the clock a hundred times that day. I was so ready to get things over with. Everything was set. David and Debbie were coming over around 6:30. David had called mom to confirm that she was going to be home for their visit. Little did she know *why* they were coming to visit.

The hour had arrived. I could hear David's car pulling up into the driveway. This was it; there was no turning back now. Things started out normal and cordial, as you could expect from any mother-son visit. We all sat down in the living room and chit-chatted awhile. But the tension was so thick that you could cut it with a knife. Finally, David said, "Mom there is a reason why we came over here today. Cheryl has got something important that she wants to tell you, and we want to be here to support her."

Mom's countenance changed drastically. She now had a look of scorned concern on her face.

All eyes were now on me. I had the floor. I told myself that I was going to be strong. But now that the moment had arrived, I knew that was a mere fantasy. I felt as if I was going to be sick. Finally, with tear-filled eyes and a shaky voice, I said, "Mom, I've got something to tell you, and you're not going to like it … I'm pregnant."

The room filled with a condemning silence. The only thing that could be heard was my sobbing. Through my tears I could see the disgusted look upon her face. She finally spoke, and I'll never forget what she said: "Well I'm not surprised. That sounds like something you would do." I was cut to the heart. I was an emotional wreck, sobbing uncontrollably.

Then, all of a sudden, David took the conversation in a direction that I didn't see coming. "Well, Mom, don't get too upset," he said. "Debbie and I have been talking, and as you know, we have been trying for years to have children, with no success. And we think we have come up with a solution that will fix everyone's problem."

"And what's that?" Mom asked in a curiously aggravated tone.

"We want to adopt Cheryl's baby."

Without hesitation, Mother said, "No, that just won't work. We're not going that route."

David seemed to be taken aback. Then he looked at me and said, "Cheryl, it's your baby. What do you think about that idea?"

I paused for a minute to gather my thoughts and my emotions, and then I said, "David, I know that you and Debbie would make great parents, but I couldn't watch my child grow up right down the road from me and not be involved in his life."

David was visibly hurt. I could tell that he had really set his heart on adopting my child. But even as immature as I was, I knew that it would just be too hard.

Mom broke the awkward silence and said, "Y'all just don't do anything. I will take care of this!" Then she stood up and walked into her bedroom, slamming the door behind her. I knew the conversation was over at that point.

The three of us sat there a minute in the silence. Then Debbie said, "David, we should probably go." David subtly shook his head in agreement, and they rose to their feet. I hugged them both and thanked them for their support. Then they walked out to their car and went on their way. I felt so bad for David. I had known that I would probably be hurt in all this, but I hadn't thought that he would get caught in the crossfire.

I went to bed that night with the weight of the world on my shoulders. The conversation had gone even worse than I'd thought it would. I was hurt, David was hurt, Mom was angry, and I still didn't have any answers. The one thing I couldn't get off my mind was what Mom had said: "I'll take care of this!" What on earth did she mean? Did she mean she would take care of this, as in, she was going to help me raise it? Or did she mean she would get me an abortion or arrange an adoption? My heart fainted within me as I pondered that question. *What did she mean?*

3
Banished

T HE TWO WEEKS THAT FOLLOWED MY confession seemed to
be rather normal on the surface. I had stopped all my partying
as soon as I suspected I was pregnant. But I continued on at my
job as a bank teller, and Mom was in and out of the house, as
usual. However, just under the surface was an almost sickening
awkwardness. She didn't speak to me much during that time, and
vice versa. Mom was definitely up to something, but I dared not
asked what. The pregnancy was the eight-hundred-pound gorilla in
the room, and we both went about life as if it wasn't there.

I became more and more anxious with each passing day. I felt
like a criminal who had just received a guilty verdict from the jury
and was now awaiting the judge's sentencing. There's not much in
life that ails me like the fear of the unknown.

Finally, Mom came into my room one night and said, "Pack
your bags. We're heading out tomorrow."

"Where are we going? And how much should I pack?" I said
with a fearful tone.

"We're going to Venice, and you'll need to pack enough to get
you through the next few months." She walked out of the room
before I could ask any more questions.

Venice, Florida, is a beach town about two hours to the south.
It's a popular vacation spot, but there was no doubt that wasn't going

to be our reason for visiting. I began to pack my things, crying every step of the way. For the past two weeks, I had been trying to get a read on Mom, attempting to figure out exactly what she thought about this whole scenario. The picture was beginning to come into focus. I didn't know exactly where I was going once I got to Venice, but it was very clear that wherever it was, Mom was leaving and I was staying there until I gave birth. I was an embarrassment to my mother, and that was obvious to me now. She wanted me out of sight, out of mind, until this whole thing was over. And what happened when the baby got here, I still didn't know.

It took me a lot longer than usual to pack, but I wasn't in any hurry. By the time I zipped up the last bag, it was late and I was exhausted. I lay down on my bed and cried myself to sleep. Ironically, sleep was the only escape from this nightmare.

It seemed like I had only shut my eyes for a few minutes when Mom stuck her head in the door and said, "Cheryl, it's time to get up. We need to leave in thirty minutes." I sat up in the bed for a minute to wipe the sleep from my eyes and attempted to pull myself out of the grogginess. I eventually rose to my feet and made my way to the bathroom. As I went to brush my teeth, I caught a glimpse of myself in the mirror. I looked like rolled-over death, and the strange thing was, I didn't really care. I had always been fairly high-maintenance, but now nothing really seemed to matter. Life as I knew it seemed to be falling apart.

I got ready and loaded my bags into the car. Mom had already started the car and was waiting for me. I let out a big sigh as I got in and buckled my seat belt, because I knew it was going to be a long ride. Mom put the car in reverse, and we backed out of the driveway and made our way onto the road.

For the first thirty minutes of the trip, neither one of us said a word. It was a deafening silence. There were so many questions I wanted to ask her, but I was afraid to. However, after a while I realized that no matter what she said or how she said it, it couldn't be worse than this horrible silence. So I finally broke the ice. "Mom, where are you taking me?"

Much to my relief, she began to answer me in a much more cordial manner than I was expecting. "Cheryl, I know that you are concerned about what's going to happen, so here is the plan. I have arranged a closed adoption for the baby. The adoption agency that we are using said that they have volunteers to take in pregnant and troubled teens. So that is why we are going to Venice."

My fear instantly turned to anger. "Troubled!" I blurted out. "What do you mean by that?"

"Well, Cheryl, it's common knowledge that you're a party girl, and now that you're pregnant, you just can't do that kind of stuff anymore."

"Mom, you know perfectly well that I haven't been anywhere but work and the house for almost two months. I'm done with that life."

"I don't *know* that," she fired back. I knew it was a cop-out.

I felt insulted, but I wasn't done asking questions yet. So I took a deep breath and started again. "So, why can't I keep the baby?"

She chuckled sarcastically and said, "Do you really want me to answer that question?"

As angry and hurt as I was, I knew she was right. I didn't have the maturity, the money, or the family structure to raise and nurture a child.

My anger left as quickly as it came, and in its place came defeat. I wanted to ask her why she wouldn't help me raise the baby, but I don't think I could have handled her answer. I truthfully don't know what she would have said, but I knew the real reason. This whole situation was embarrassing to Mom, and she wanted to get it over with and put it behind her. I quietly sat back in the seat and dropped the conversation.

At this point, some readers might be asking themselves *why*.

Why didn't I fight for the baby? Why didn't I move out or get another job or do whatever it took to raise my child? After all, I was nineteen. I have spent the majority of my life agonizing over those very same questions. Could I, or should I, have done anything different? The truth is, I was immature, weak, selfish, and simply incapable, and I hated myself for it. That was just the way it was, and all the speculation in the world won't change the decisions that were made.

As we neared our final destination, Mom began to brief me on the specifics of where she was taking me. "Miss Ridley is affiliated with the adoption agency, and she has agreed to take you in until you deliver. You will be under her supervision at all times. She is a single mother of two small children, and it's very generous of her to take you in, so you need to show her the utmost respect. This isn't a vacation, so don't treat it like one." Mom's words were just a distant echo at this point. What I thought and what I wanted had no relevance. I was just along for the ride.

The next four months were both agonizing and uneventful. Miss Ridley and her children were sweet people, but they were total strangers. I was living with total strangers, two hours away from home, at this extremely difficult time in my life. I had no money and no car, and I was always under constant supervision. For the first two weeks, I hardly ate or slept, and I begged Mom every day over the phone to come and get me, but she never did. I had been banished, and there was no way out.

I have found, however, that in almost every situation in life there *is* a silver lining. The silver lining in all this was that I was forced to grow up. I had an awful lot of time to think, and I was made to take an honest look at my life and my mistakes. Whoever said, "What doesn't kill you makes you stronger," was absolutely right. When you are faced with adverse circumstances that are completely out of your control, it *will* refine you.

I had been at the Ridley's for about three and a half months when, out of the blue, Mom called me and said, "Pack your bags. I'm coming to get you."

I was elated. Perhaps she'd had a change of heart! But it wasn't so. For some reason, Mother had decided to change adoption agencies. She picked me up in Venice and drove me to Gainesville, which is about two hours north of home. Once again she dropped me off with total strangers, and once again I was left to my thoughts. However, this time it was easier. I don't know if it was because I was stronger or had become numb to the circumstances or if it was because I was due soon. I think it was because, in a three-and-a-half-month period, I had become a different person. I had come to an honest place of remorse and regret over my sins. I had also, to some extent, come to grips with the reality of the situation.

I was only three weeks away from my due date when Mom took me to the Scotts' home. They were a picture of the stereotypical American Dream. Mr. and Mrs. Scott were in their thirties and had two young children, a boy and a girl. They had a large back yard with a lot of playground equipment for the kids. It seemed like they were out there with their kids every day. I would sit outside and read, while they played with their kids in the backyard. It was a bittersweet experience, watching the joy they shared as a family. Just seeing the happiness it brought them to swing their daughter in the swing or to help their son across the monkey bars was almost enough to bring me to tears. It was a sobering reminder that giving my child up for adoption was the right thing to do. I didn't see how I could ever hope to give him what the Scotts gave their children.

It's almost impossible to describe how it felt to know that I was going to have to give up my child. Every mother who has ever carried a child loves them before they are even born—so much that they can't wait to meet them. I felt the same way, but I loved mine so much that I had to let him go. I know that seems like an oxymoron, but giving him up for adoption was the most loving thing I could have done for my child. I *was* doing the right thing. At least that's what I kept telling myself.

I had been at the Scotts' house for almost three weeks when it happened. On the night of November 8, 1984, I went to bed just like I had every night. But at about two o'clock in the morning, I was awakened by the unmistakable pains of labor. Now that the moment was finally here, I was in shock. I can't describe the mixture of joy and sadness that I felt at that time. For the past nine months it had seemed like a bad dream, but now it was a full-fledged reality. No time to mope now. It was go time.

4
Labor Day

**A woman when she is in travail hath sorrow, because
her hour is come: but as soon as she is delivered of the
child, she remembereth no more the anguish, for joy
that a man is born into the world.**
—John 16:21

A S SOON AS I REALIZED WHAT was happening, I got out of bed, got dressed, and made my way to the Scotts' bedroom. I gently knocked on the door and whispered, "Mrs. Scott."

Within a few seconds, she opened the door and said, "Is everything all right, Cheryl?"

"I'm having some really strong contractions. I think it might be time," I replied, trying not to seem too dramatic. But I think it was obvious to her that I was in a lot of pain.

"Let me throw some clothes on, and I'll drive you to the hospital," she said in a concerned voice.

In just a few minutes, she reappeared, softly shutting the door behind her. We quietly navigated our way through the dark house as we headed for the garage. I walked around the car to the passenger side and very gingerly sat down in the seat, shutting the door behind me. The pain seemed to be intensifying by the minute. Mrs. Scott backed the car out of the driveway and onto the road in a hurried manner. Thankfully, the hospital wasn't a far drive from the Scott home.

When we arrived at Alachua General Hospital, she pulled around to the ER entrance. She put the car in park and told me to wait there and that she would get someone to bring a wheelchair out to the car. In no time, they were wheeling me down the hallway to the women's center. They took me straight to a room, gave me a gown to change into, and said, "The nurse will be in to see you shortly." I went into the bathroom and changed, and as I opened the door and walked into the room, I could see Mrs. Scott sitting in the corner. I was glad that she was staying with me, even though I had only known her a few weeks. At least I wouldn't be totally alone.

No sooner had I lain down in the bed than the nurse came in to examine me and check the baby's vitals. "Well it's definitely time," she said very matter-of-factly as she began to prepare an IV. "I'm assuming you want an epidural?"

"Oh, please do," I replied without hesitation. I honestly don't know how the women of old used to do it, and I sure didn't have any plans for finding out. Not long after the nurse left, the anesthesiologist came in, and after a shot in both hips, I was feeling much, *much* better.

Now that I was all hooked up and medicated, the waiting game began. Thanks to the epidural, the physical pain had subsided, but the absence of pain now allowed my mind to wander freely. The grim reality of the situation began to assert itself. Those ten hours of labor are an experience that I will never forget. It's hard to put into words the melting pot of emotions that I was feeling at that time. As Charles Dickens so eloquently put it, "It was the best of times; it was the worst of times."

Under normal circumstances, childbirth is one of the most precious and joyous occasions that a family, and especially a mother, can experience. And in many ways my pregnancy was no different. In fact, the anticipation period was exactly the same as for any mother. I had carried my child for nine months. I had heard his heartbeat on the ultrasound. I'd felt him kick in my belly. I'd felt it when he had the hiccups. He had been a part of me for all that time. And despite all of the outside circumstances, he was *my* child. Sadly, however, this was where it would have to end. The horrible reality was that all of the normalcy, all of the love, and all of the motherly instincts had to go out the window as soon as my son was born into the world.

The next ten hours were a gloomy revelation of just how sad the situation was. There was no family waiting in the lobby to meet my newborn. There were no balloons that told the world, "It's a Boy!" There was no first outfit for the baby to wear. No, there was nothing normal about this delivery. To make things worse, the nurses kept it extremely dark in the room, and although they remained professional about their duties, they hardly spoke to me at all. I don't know if they felt bad for me or if they were passing judgment. Perhaps they just didn't know what to say.

The hours dragged on, and nothing much changed until about eleven o'clock the next morning. Mom finally walked in to relieve Mrs. Scott about the time that things got serious. That final hour of labor was exasperating. I pushed and breathed and pushed and breathed until I thought I couldn't do it anymore. Finally, the doctor said, "I can see the head. Just one more big push." I closed my eyes so tightly that it hurt. I made up my mind that no matter what happened, I wasn't going to open them. Seeing my son right before they took him away would be more than I could bear. I took a deep breath, and with all my might, I pushed one last time. And into the world he came.

I had shut my eyes, but I couldn't turn off my hearing. There isn't a word in the English dictionary that's powerful enough to describe the intense range of emotion I felt when I heard him crying less than three feet away from me. I felt such love, and yet, such despair. I remember asking the doctor if he was all right.

"Yes, ma'am, he's a healthy baby boy," he said. No sooner had those words come out of his mouth than I heard my son's cry leave the room and fade down the hallway until I couldn't hear him anymore. The room filled with a dead silence. From the time he was born until the time he was gone couldn't have been longer than ninety seconds.

This precious moment had finally come, and almost instantly, it was gone. I remember shouting, "God, what have I done? What have I done!" I was supposed to be holding him and talking to him. I was supposed to be welcoming him into the world. I was supposed to be kissing him and letting him know that he was loved. But now I didn't even know where he was or who he was with. I had no clue as to his future. I didn't get to name him. I didn't even get to see him. How many mothers can say that they've never even seen their own child?

I just lay there and sobbed until my eyes burned. I remember my mom holding my hand during that time, which was a huge gesture for her. Showing affection didn't come easy for her. Perhaps she was having second thoughts as well. But all of that was little consolation now. There was absolutely nothing that could be done.

A few hours went by before one of the nurses came into the room. "Miss Heath, we're going to move you to another room to recover, if that's okay with you." I nodded nonchalantly. What did it matter? She brought a wheelchair in, and they took me to a totally different part of the hospital. I was glad, because I didn't really want to be around all of the new mothers with their babies. Perhaps this was what the nurses had in mind at the time.

I lay down on the bed in my new room, exhausted in every way possible. I was so tired, but I couldn't sleep. I felt like the scum of the earth. I had failed my son. But then again, I *had* done the right thing, hadn't I? That was the one question that kept burning in my mind. I lay there, lifeless, and the only way I know to describe how I felt is: *empty*. I felt like a part of me died that day, and in a way, it had.

Somehow, I managed to finally fall asleep. I catnapped my way through the night and into the next morning. When I awoke, the pain and emptiness started right where it had left off. I lay there quietly all morning, until the nurse came in and said, "Well you're ready to go home." Those words were music to my ears. It's easier to suffer at home than anywhere else on earth.

Mom said, "I'll go pull the car up," and she walked out the door. The nurse helped me into the wheelchair. She turned me around to face the door, and to my surprise, instead of pushing me into the hallway, she walked in front of me and shut the door. It was just me and her in the room now. She looked at me and said, "Look, I know it's been a traumatic couple of days for you, and I want to give you something." I looked at her with a puzzled look as she spoke. "Before I give it to you, though, you have to promise me that you won't say anything about it, because I could get into a lot of trouble for doing this."

I nodded and said, "Don't worry. I won't tell."

She reached into her pocket and pulled out a Polaroid of my son. She handed it to me and said, "I thought you should have something to remember him by." Through tear-filled eyes, I saw my beautiful son, his head full of hair. I thanked her as best I could, although I don't know if my words were discernable through all of my emotion. She handed me some tissue and gave me a minute to regroup. She then proceeded to wheel me to the exit door, where Mom was waiting in the car. I never forgot the kindness that nursed extended to me that day.

Mom drove me home. She had been with me most of the time since she had arrived at the hospital. She hadn't said much at all during this time, and neither had I. What *could* we say?

When I arrived home, I went straight to my room, shut my door, and lay down on the bed. I felt so numb. I had no ambition, no desire, and no life. Every day I was tormented by the same questions: Where was he? Was he being taken care of? Had he been placed with a loving family, or was he in some orphanage somewhere? Did I do the right thing? These same questions would haunt me for the next twenty-seven years.

For about two weeks, I barely ate or slept. I hardly left my room, and if I was awake, I was crying. The closest thing I can compare it to is the tragic and unexpected death of a loved one. I was in a grieving process, and there was no quick fix. However, after the first two weeks I seemed to get a little stronger. I could at least eat and sleep a little bit, and I began to get out of my room for a while. But for the first two months, I didn't leave the house at all, unless it was to run errands for Mom.

After two months had come and gone, something happened, something I never thought I would live to see. The human mind, as well as the human body, is truly a miraculous creation, and it has an amazing way of healing itself. I had grieved until I couldn't grieve any more. I had cried until I couldn't cry anymore. And one morning I woke up and felt as if I had been healed. I felt so good, but at the same time I felt guilty, as if somehow I was forgetting about my son. I knew that some scars would never completely heal. I also knew that I would never forget about my son. But right or wrong, that morning when I woke up, I knew that I was ready to move on with my life.

5
Life Goes On

WHEN I FINALLY GOT ON MY feet again, one of the very first things I did was go out and look for a job. In February of 1985 I was hired by State Farm. This marked the start of my new life. I never went back to the old friends or to the party scene. I had experienced the painful consequences firsthand, and I wanted no part of it.

Over the next twenty-seven years, life moved on. In June of 1986, I was married, and a year later, my husband and I welcomed our first child into the world. He was a beautiful baby boy. We named him Devin.

I could tell very quickly that the horrific experience I'd had with my first child was going to affect my parenting. When Devin was born, I remember how tightly I clung to him. I didn't even let the nurse take him to the nursery. I wasn't letting go this time.

Two years later, I gave birth to our second son, Forrest. Two years after that, I gave birth to our baby girl, Amber. When they were born, I was just as protective over them, not allowing them to be taken to the nursery.

Not long after Amber was born, my first husband and I were divorced. That was a tough time for me. I had three young children to take care of and hardly any means by which to do it. It gave me a much greater appreciation for the way my mom had worked to provide for me and my brothers when she became a single mother.

I had been divorced about a year when I met the man that would become my second husband: Ronnie Culpepper. I'd never thought that I would find a good man who would be willing to marry a single mother of three. But Ronnie was just that man. I really believed that he would have taken the shirt off his back to help me and the kids, and I still believe that today. We were married in July of 1993, and together we raised the kids.

That period of my life when the kids were growing up was a time that I will always cherish. For the first time in my life, I felt loved, I felt needed, and my children were my pride and joy. My children were and always will be my heartbeat. I loved getting to know them as they grew and transformed into the people that they are today.

My children are all different, both in their looks and their personalities. Devin has such a good heart. He is the type of person who couldn't sleep if he knew that he had hurt someone's feelings that day. He is very good with computers and is currently an IT man with Publix.   Forrest is a very determined person and a poetic soul. He has been blessed with a great musical gift. He plays several instruments, but my favorite is when he plays the violin. Amber is so full of energy, it's hard to keep up with her. She is a sweetheart and the brains in the family. She is currently studying for a degree in Psychology at the University of Central Florida.

When I think of the children growing up, it always brings a mixed bag of emotions for me. It was such a joy sharing those "moments" with them, those moments that grip the heart of every parent: their first words, first steps, losing their first tooth, Christmas, birthdays, and so on. On the other hand, it was a constant reminder for me that somebody else would be sharing those special moments with my first son.

I had determined early on, however, that I wasn't going to try and find him. Don't get me wrong; I wanted nothing more than to find him and bring him home. But I felt like I had signed away my rights as a mother. After all, what right did I have to go barging into his life and the lives of his family?

Twenty-seven years came and went—over a quarter of a century—and there wasn't a single day that went by that I didn't think about my son. There were some days that were better than others. But there were certain things that would stir up all those feelings and emotions—certain songs, movies, and places. The hardest time, however, was always at night, when everything was quiet and I was lying in bed trying to go to sleep. That's when the past came rushing back to me as if it had just happened the day before. As horrible as it is to experience the death of a loved one, at least there is a sense of closure. I never felt any of that closure when it came to my son.

Many times when people lose a close relative, they have a certain day of the year when they take time to visit the grave site and reflect on their memories. I didn't have a grave to visit, but every year on my son's birthday, I would have to get off by myself. It was a reminder of another year that had come and gone. It killed me to know that somewhere in the world there was a happy family gathered together in a room full of balloons and party hats, watching my son blow out the candles on the cake.

Through the years I had learned to suppress my feelings, and although I had told Ronnie about the adoption even before we were married, I never told my children. I guess if I was honest with myself, it was partly because I was afraid of what they might think of me. But I think the biggest reason I didn't tell them was because I knew they would have worried about their brother, even having never met him. They would have felt obligated to find him, and I didn't want them to have to bear that burden.

There is an old saying that "time heals all wounds," but strangely enough, my pain got *worse* over time. As I said before, when the kids were growing up, I had many reminders of my first son. But when the kids grew up and moved out, it was a lot worse.

Deep in my heart, I had always hoped that my son would find me. However, I didn't even know for sure if he knew that he was adopted or not. But I felt that if he *did* know, the best odds of him finding me would be in his young adult years. I had always figured that before that time he wouldn't have the means to find me, and if he waited until after his young adult years, it would be because he didn't want to find me.

The heartache and longing got worse and worse, and on January 29, 2012, it seemed like it had reached new heights. It was my forty-seventh birthday, and I remember lying there in bed next to Ronnie that night, just thinking about my son. I guess it was because my birthday served as a sobering reminder of how many years had passed. My son would have been twenty-seven years old, and if my theory was correct, if he didn't find me soon, then he probably never would.

As I lay there, I began to unload my feelings on Ronnie as I had so many times before. I said, "Ronnie, do you think he'll ever find me? Do you think he even knows?" And he began to try and comfort me as he had many times in the past. "I'm sure he will someday, and worrying about it won't make it happen any faster."

"I know, but I can't help but wonder where he is or what he looks like. Is he happy? What's his name? I wonder if and when he will ever find me?" Little did I know what was about to happen.

6
A World Apart: Brandon's Story

Therefore if any man be in Christ, he is a new creature:
old things are passed away; behold, all things are
become new."
—2 Corinthians 5:17

IF SOMEONE HAD SEEN MY FAMILY, they wouldn't have noticed that anything was different. If they had looked through our family photo album, they would have seen baby pictures of me playing with my sister Brooke. My birth certificate reads, parents: Gary and Glenda Vaughan. But as soon as I was old enough to understand, they explained to me that I had been adopted.

As I got a little older, my parents went into further detail about how they had adopted me from an agency in Gainesville, Florida, when I was two months old. I was in foster care for the first two months, while they waded through all the red tape of an intrastate adoption. They had tried to have children of their own for years but had been unsuccessful. Mom even gave birth to stillborn twin boys. So they began the laborious process of adoption. Ironically, not long before the adoption was final, my mother found out that she was pregnant with my sister. But at that point, they had already set their hearts on bringing me home, and in January of 1985, they flew to Gainesville to pick me up.

They took me to their home in Columbus, Mississippi. We lived

29

there for about two years, until Dad changed jobs and we moved to Memphis. We weren't there but about a year and Dad got another job in Tuscaloosa, Alabama. I was four years old when we moved to Tuscaloosa, and I've been here ever since. I guess it will always be the place that I call home.

Being adopted really didn't affect me that much as a child. I felt like I had a perfectly "normal" life. Dad worked as a car salesman, and Mom stayed home to raise me and Brooke. Although Brooke was their biological child, I never felt like they favored or loved her more than me. Brooke and I had people tell us all the time that we favored one another, and because we were so close in age, we were often mistaken for twins. We were always in the same grade in school growing up, which I thought was pretty cool. We used to crack up at the reactions and double takes we got when we told people that we were nine months apart. They must have thought that Mom was the bionic woman.

I couldn't have imagined a happier childhood. I did all of the normal things that kids do. For the first six years that we were in Tuscaloosa, we lived in the rural Duncanville community, so we had a lot of woods around our house. It seemed like I was outside with the neighbor's kids all the time, playing hide-and-seek and riding bikes. We had a steep hill behind our house, and one of my favorite things to do was to swing down the hill on tree vines. I also liked to spend the night with friends and vice versa. We would stay up half the night playing video games.

My Dad and I are huge Alabama football fans. I guess it's unavoidable, growing up in Tuscaloosa. Some of my fondest memories growing up were when he took me to the football games to cheer on the Crimson Tide along with ninety thousand other fans.

We were also heavily involved in church. My dad was raised in the Church of Christ, and so he attempted to carry on the tradition with me and Brooke. We were in church almost every time the doors were open: Sunday school, Sunday morning and evening services, Wednesday night service, Vacation Bible School—you name it, and we were there.

When I was in the fourth grade, we moved across town to the blooming suburb of Taylorville in the newly constructed neighborhood of Englewood Meadows. It kind of reminded me of the "Leave It to Beaver" community. There were so many neighborhood kids that were around my age. It seemed like every day we were in a different yard playing tackle football. We thought we were so tough. And when we weren't playing football, we would ride our bikes to the school ballpark about a half a mile away, where we would play home-run derby.

For the most part, I was a "golden child" while growing up. I made As and Bs on my report card, said *ma'am* and *sir*, and, although I was extremely strong-willed, I tried to use it for the good. However, when I got into middle school, I made some bad friends, and they rubbed off on me terribly. I was an extremely shy and introverted person, and I think I enjoyed being around them because they were somewhat of outcasts, and I didn't feel like they were judging me. They were also very good at bringing me out of my shell. My early teen years marked some major changes in my life, most of them for the worst, but one of them for the best.

It first started with music. My friends introduced me to the rising scene of grunge and punk rock. I absolutely idolized the bands that we listened to. It was during this time that I began learning to play guitar. I wanted to be just like my favorite bands. I was looking through some of my yearbooks recently and found it somewhat comical that in one of my middle school pictures I was wearing a Green Day T-shirt. Most people don't think a lot about music, but with it comes both a message and a lifestyle. I was too naïve to understand that at the time.

When I was thirteen, I was introduced to a whole lot more than just music. It was then that I felt a lot of my innocence was stolen. One weekend I went to a friend's house. Two of my friends and I were all just sitting around watching TV, when one of their dads came home from work.

"What are y'all watchin'," he said in his typical friendly tone.

"Nothin' much," we replied with our usual answer.

"You boys wanna see somethin' good?"

"Sure," we said. We weren't really into anything anyway.

He walked into his bedroom for a minute, and when he came back out, he said to us, "Now boys, don't go home and tell your mommies about this. This here is big boy stuff." I had no clue what he was talking about at the time, but I found out real quick when he put the tape into the VCR. There I sat, at thirteen years old, watching pornography with two of my friends and one of their fathers.

I'm not even sure that I could accurately explain what those images did to my young mind. And even if I could, I probably wouldn't want to. At thirteen, I was a lot more child than I was adult. I would like to be able to say that it was a onetime thing, but the truth is that from that point on there probably wasn't a single time when we were at that house that we didn't watch it. It messed with my mind, to say the least. Pornography is a drug, just like meth and crack, and it has some deep-seated effects.

It was during this time that I dealt with a lot of guilt for the things that were going on in my life. I had never had anyone look me in the eye and point-blank tell me that they were wrong, but in my heart, I knew. I knew that my mother would be disappointed if she knew about the music lyrics I listened to, the videos I watched, and the language I used. I had a mouth that would make a sailor blush. I know that there are plenty of people who will read this book and think that all of that was nothing, but at the age of thirteen, it couldn't have been a good omen of things to come.

I began to look to religion for answers. Not long after my fourteenth birthday, in December of 1998, I went to a retreat in

Birmingham with our Church of Christ youth group. One night after the minister had finished his message, he invited anyone who wanted to go to heaven to come down and be baptized. I thought to myself, "That's exactly what I need."

So I made my way down to the front, all the way down from the balcony, to profess my decision, and later that night I was baptized in the pool at the hotel where we were staying. But there was no change in my life at all. I didn't feel any different, and my actions didn't change. The old saying about baptism is, "Down with the old man and up with the new." But with me it was, "Down with the old man and up with the wet old man." I remember thinking to myself, *Is this all there is to it?* I'm so glad to report that there is a whole lot more to the Lord than that.

Six months later, in June of 1999, a friend from school invited me to an outing with his church youth group. There wasn't much to it. We went out to eat and played kickball behind the church, but I saw something in the youth pastor and in most of the youth members that just seemed different to me. I couldn't explain it, but they seemed to have a peace that I wanted. They invited me to come to church the following morning, and I agreed. After all, the church was less than a mile from my house.

It was the last Sunday in June of 1999 when I walked into Englewood Baptist Church. During Sunday school, the youth pastor, Brother Mark Rice, preached the true gospel to me for the first time in my life. He told us about the Lord Jesus coming to earth to die on the cross for our sins, that He rose from the dead on the third day, and that He is alive today, seated at the right hand of the Father. He told us that if we would repent and put our trust in Him, that He would forgive us of our sins and give us eternal life.

I could feel the Spirit of the Lord pulling at my heart. I had such a feeling of conviction rush over me. It was the first time in my life that I saw myself as a sinner in need of a savior. After class was over, I ran out of the room and made my way to the sanctuary for the morning service. The worship service just further intensified my conviction, as Brother Bill Richards also presented a strong, clear dose of the Gospel. There had to have been four or five hundred people there that morning, but I felt like he was preaching directly to me. I was so ready to get out of that place.

After the service was over, Brother Mark came up to me. He could obviously tell that I was under conviction. He point-blank asked me if I was saved. "Yeah, I've been baptized," I said. I think he knew that I didn't really want to talk about it, so he merely invited me back to church and left it at that.

I might have left the church building that day, but the conviction never left me. That whole week, I was miserable. For those who have never experienced Holy Ghost conviction, it's difficult to explain, other than that it is as real as the heartbeat in your chest. I told the Lord that if He would let me live long enough to get back to church the next Sunday that I would give my life to Him. I was too spiritually illiterate to understand that I didn't have to be in church to get saved.

Sunday finally came, and as soon as Sunday school was over, I grabbed Brother Mark and told him that I needed to know how to be saved. I couldn't even wait for the service to start. It was on that day, July 4, 1999, that I gave my life to the Lord in the youth room at Englewood Baptist Church, and I have never been the same. The grass seemed greener, the sky seemed a lighter shade of blue, and it felt as if the weight of the world had been lifted off of my shoulders. I knew that I had found the meaning of life, and from that day on, I wanted to serve the Lord. The songwriter Alfred Ackley worded it best when he said, "You ask me how I know He lives. He lives within my heart." There is no doubt that through the years I have failed Him many times, but I can honestly say that He has never once failed me.

I went home that day and tore down all of the band posters in my room. I also went out to the backyard and played Frisbee with my CD collection. I had no desire to listen to them anymore. They no longer spoke my language. I also parted ways with my old friends. It's not that I did away with them; it's just that they didn't want to be around me anymore, because I had become a "religious nut."

That same month, I was baptized again—this time for the right reasons. This time my baptism was a symbol of my salvation instead of the *vehicle* of my salvation. It was merely a wedding ring to showcase the marriage that had taken place between Christ and me. I then became a member of Englewood Baptist Church and began to serve the Lord there. I turned into an incessant student of the Word during this time. I had such a burning desire to grow and learn. Even as a young Christian, I believed that God had a purpose for my life, and I wanted to discover what it was.

Yes, I had a life of my own. And as far as my past was concerned, all I knew was that I had been born in Gainesville, Florida, in November of 1984. Being adopted was simply a nonfactor for me growing up. It's just not something that I thought a whole lot about. I knew that out there, *somewhere*, I had a biological mother and father. They could have been right down the street for all I knew, but as far as my life was concerned, they were a world apart. Little did I know how drastically that would change in the years to come.

7

An Empty Past

M Y HIGH SCHOOL YEARS WERE A special time for me in many ways. It was a time filled with both fond memories and great transition. To start with, I had made some new friends at church who were like brothers to me: Brett Morrison and Mike (Bubba) McCool.

It was an interesting friendship. We enjoyed a lot of the same hobbies, but our personalities were like night and day in comparison. I was a serious, no-nonsense kind of guy, while Brett and Bubba, well, they were the class clowns. Brett reminded me of a country version of Jim Carrey. He could make me laugh on the saddest day of my life. He was the type of person who, if we pulled up next to a total stranger at a red light, could wave at them with such excitement and emotion that the stranger would feel obligated to smile and wave back, thinking that Brett must know them. No doubt they drove away saying to themselves, "Who was *that* guy?"

Bubba, on the other hand, was more of the silent, sly type. His childhood nickname was deceiving; he was actually very intelligent. He was what I would call a passive agitator, because he loved to play mind games with people. Bubba had a subtle way of making people feel self-conscious. For example, he could stare at you in a certain way that made you feel as if you had a cow lick or had missed a spot while shaving that morning. And no matter how many times he did it to me, I *always* fell for it and had to go find a mirror. It always made his day too.

Yes, I was the DB, the Designated Babysitter, making sure that they didn't hurt themselves or anyone else. On the other hand, their mission in life was to get me out of both my shell and my comfort zone at all costs. Together we made a great team. When I think of our friendship, I think of what Ecclesiastes 4:12 says: "A threefold cord is not quickly broken."

For several years we were almost inseparable. If we weren't out with the youth group or at each other's house, we were out hunting or fishing. We even went on family vacations together to places like Orange Beach, Alabama, and Pigeon Forge, Tennessee. Their parents were like parents to me. They often joked about me being their "other" son. At one point we all had keys to each other's houses and an "open-door policy" to use them. We were just that close.

One of our favorite things to do was to head out to our getaway spot about an hour's drive south, where Bubba's parents had a little camp house on the Tom Bigbee River. We loved to go down there for days at a time to hunt or go jug fishing. It was great just to get away from everything and everyone for a while.

We also ended up at the same school together. After I got saved, I just didn't seem to fit in or feel comfortable in the public school environment. So my parents graciously allowed me to transfer my freshman year to Tuscaloosa Christian School across town. It was a small school. I only had twenty-one people in my class, but I loved it. Brett had already been attending there for several years, because his mother was a teacher there. Bubba also transferred there the year after I did. On top of everything else, we were in the same school and on the same baseball and football teams.

In so many ways, life was better than it had ever been. I was saved, I had a good church and good friends, and I was in a good school. Yet other areas of my life were changing drastically, and not for the better. At home, things had taken a turn for the worst. Dad was making some incredibly irresponsible choices, and as a result, my parents' marriage was on the rocks. My relationship with my dad suffered greatly during that time. I didn't want to be around him, and I didn't really like being at home. I was so thankful to be able to go out and be with my friends during that time. It was an escape from harsh reality.

It was also during this time that I began to go through that mid-teen transition that every person goes through: that period of transformation between an adolescent and a young adult. The teenage years are hard on everyone in some way or another. Between dealing with school, peer pressure, and trying to find out who you are, it can be tough. Everyone goes through that phase of trying to "find themselves," but for me that seemed to take on a whole new meaning. I just seemed to have more questions to answer than the average person.

I was about fifteen when I really began to have questions about my past. I had never really given it much thought up until that point, and it all started with the small stuff. I would look into the mirror and wonder where I got my blue eyes or my incredibly straight hair. Whom did I get my personality traits from?

It started small enough, but over time I began to think more deeply on the subject, and the questions became a lot more intense. Where were my parents? Why had they given me away? What had happened? Did they love me? I wondered if they ever thought about me. The lack of answers to these questions troubled me deeply—so deeply, in fact, that I had to open up and talk to Mom about it, which was a miracle in itself. I'm a shy and closed-off person by nature. So talking to Mom about something as deep and troubling to me as the adoption was a rare feat.

It may seem rather unbelievable, but the first time in my life that I really sat down with Mom and had a serious, involved conversation about the adoption was when I was fifteen. I just went up to her one day while she was unloading the dishwasher and asked her what she knew about my birth parents. "I really don't know anything about them, Bran," she said, using her nickname for me. "Closed adoption is a very secretive thing. On one end, we contacted the adoption agency, wanting to adopt; and on the other end, your birth parents contacted the agency, wanting to give you up for adoption. Everything was done through a mediator."

"So you don't know anything about them at all?" I asked dejectedly.

At that moment, Mom walked into the laundry room to the shelf where she kept all the important files. She reached into the small, black filing cabinet and pulled out a folder labeled "adoption." She opened it up and pulled out a packet of three or four stapled pieces of paper and handed it to me. "This is all that we have of your past, son." I looked down at the papers she handed me. The top line read: "Family History." My heart began to accelerate in my chest as I read those words. Could this be my link to the past?

As I read those typed words, I was filled with both excitement and disappointment. There was no identifying information, nothing that I could use to find my birth parents. But at the same time, I was looking at some information on my family for the first time. I found out that my mother was about five foot six with blonde, straight hair and that she liked to ride horses. My father was my exact size: about six feel tall, 170 pounds, medium build. It also said that he liked to ride motorcycles. The papers also listed some physical characteristics about my birth mother's family—uncles, grandparents, etc. But it wasn't nearly enough to satisfy my curiosity. In fact, it just left me feeling frustrated.

I think seeing those papers that day did me more harm than good. It left me with more questions than answers. "Why would they give me away? Who could give up their own child? Why did I seem to be the only person who didn't know *anything* about his past? I think it's just human nature that, when we don't have the facts, we tend to assume the worst. And so in my mind, the answers to those questions seemed too painful to bear. I had an empty past and only negative assumptions to fill it with. It's amazing to think that I had such a "normal" life and yet was so troubled by a void in my past, but that's just the way that it was.

I handed the papers back to Mom and thanked her for showing them to me. She could tell that I was upset as she said, "I'm sorry. I don't have anything else on them, but I'm sure that they loved you. I'm sure that they felt like they had to give you away." I heard what she said, but the wisdom of those words went in one ear and out the other. From that point on, I made up my mind that, since I didn't have any way of getting answers, I wasn't going to torment myself with any more questions. I just wasn't going to think or talk about the subject anymore. Case closed.

So that was exactly what I did. I pushed it out of my mind and just didn't think about it, and it seemed to work quite well. For a period of almost two years, I *willed* it to become a nonfactor, as it had been in my childhood. However, one day those walls I had built came crashing to the ground.

8
Every Life

**But God hath chosen the foolish things of the world
to confound the wise; and God hath chosen the weak
things of the world to confound the things which are
mighty.**
—1 Corinthians 1:27

IT WAS MY SENIOR YEAR OF high school in the fall of 2002. I
remember sitting in Mr. McQueen's Bible class, feeling absolutely
miserable. Something had been eating at me for weeks, and up until
the night before, I'd had no clue what it was.

For quite a while I had been burdened about family members
and classmates that hadn't been saved. It's sad to think that a
Christian school can have a large number of non-Christians in it,
but it's just reality. I worried about their salvation and their eternal
destination so much that I even began to have dreams about it.
I had dreams about people I knew, dying and going to hell, and
from the flames they screamed for me to help them. When I woke
up, I remember thinking to myself that someone should tell them
the truth of the gospel. That's when the Lord spoke to my heart
and said, "Why don't *you* tell them?" Of course, I didn't hear Him
audibly, but I heard Him just the same. God was calling me to
preach His Word.

Now don't get me wrong. I don't put any stock in dreams or

prophesies or any form of extra-biblical revelation. I believe that my dreams were simply a result of me thinking about the subject throughout the day. But I *do* believe that God used them to make me realize that He was calling me into the ministry. I felt like the Lord wanted me to start by giving my testimony at one of our school chapel services. But I really didn't want to.

Being a preacher isn't a vocation; it's a calling. The call to preach was as real to me as the call to salvation. It was something I couldn't push aside, and I was going to be miserable until I said, "Yes, Lord." The only problem was that I didn't want to say yes. After all, how could *I*, a shy, seventeen-year-old, be a preacher? How could I stand before my peers and give my testimony? The thought to me was both terrifying and laughable.

I wasn't going to do it, and that was all there was to it. I was too young and too shy. And then I came up with the greatest excuse of all: I was an accident who wasn't even supposed to be here. It wasn't that I wouldn't do it; I *couldn't* do it. That sounded a whole lot better, anyway. As all of the other students sat quietly and did their bookwork, there was a war raging inside of me. I was having myself a good old-fashioned pity party from my second-row desk.

As I sat there, I began to dwell on the thought that had just popped into my head. Was I *really* an accident, simply an unwanted consequence of an irresponsible act? I mean, if my parents had planned me, wouldn't they have kept me? Those walls I had built up came crashing to the ground with this one, heart-wrenching thought. I was at a great crossroad in my thought process. If I *was* an accident, then what did that say about my purpose in life, my future, or my destiny? Did God really have a plan for my life, or was it just something that I'd come up with on my own?

I went back and forth in my mind, until I did the only thing that I knew to do. I got out my Bible and opened it up. I would say that I randomly turned to Jeremiah, chapter one, but the truth is that it *couldn't* have been an accident. Jeremiah was a young prophet whom scholars believed was in his teens when God called him to preach judgment to the backslidden nation of Israel. In chapter one, God called Jeremiah to preach His Word, and like me, Jeremiah said to the Lord, "I cannot speak: for I am a child." I was amazed that of all the places I could have turned to, I came across this incident with Jeremiah. I could certainly relate to what he was going through. But it was when I took a second look at verse five that both my thinking and my life were changed.

The Lord told Jeremiah in chapter one, verse five, "Before I formed thee in the belly I knew thee; and before thou camest forth out of the womb I sanctified thee, and ordained thee a prophet unto the nations." I was absolutely dumbfounded as I read that verse. Those three words, "I formed thee," forever changed the way I looked at both my life and the adoption. I realized that God had just as much to do with me being here as my parents did, and that had to mean that He really *did* have a plan for my life!

Students are taught in biology class that it takes two people to conceive a child, but I have learned that it takes three. In our finite minds, we can't even begin to understand the sovereignty of God. But I *do* know that without the hand of God being involved, the miracle of child conception would be impossible. Scientists, with all of their knowledge and technology, will never be able to clone or create a living, breathing, functioning human being. The best that they can ever hope to do is to copy and paste the genetic code that God has already made. However, they cannot give man a living soul.

I once heard a story about a scientist who wanted to prove that he was as wise and powerful as God is. So he walked up to the top of a tall hill and called out for God to show Himself. The Lord appeared unto the man and asked him to speak his peace. The scientist said to Lord, "I heard that you created man from the dust of the earth."

"That's right," the Lord replied.

"Well I'm here to show you that I can do it too," said the scientist.

"Go right ahead," said the Lord.

The scientist bent down and began to pile and shape the dirt into the form of a man. He hadn't gotten very far when the Lord said, "What are you doing?"

"I'm making a man out of the dirt, just like you."

To this the Lord replied, "Well, first of all, you need to find your own dirt." It's not the most well-founded example in the world, but it sure is true.

As the days went on, I dug deeper into the subject, and I found out that the Bible is full of information about God's hand in conception. In Genesis 1:27, the Bible tells us that in the original creation God created man in His image. We were created to reflect Him. What a privilege! What a responsibility! We are like the moon, which has no light of itself, but it becomes beautiful when it reflects the light from the sun. The Lord equips every person born into the world with their own special talents, personalities, and qualities with which to glorify Him. In the case of Jeremiah, the Lord ordained him to be a prophet unto the nations while he was yet in the womb.

This may seem hard to believe, but Exodus 4:11 reveals that God is even responsible for making the deaf, dumb, and blind. God can even get glory from those with undesirable infirmities. In John 1:1–3, the Lord Jesus got glory from a man who was blind from birth. When His disciples saw the blind man, they asked Jesus, "Master, who did sin, this man, or his parents, that he was born blind?" Jesus answered, "Neither hath this man sinned, nor his parents: but that the works of God should be made manifest in Him."

There is a young man in our church whom everyone calls John-John. He has cerebral palsy, but he loves to sing for the Lord. John-John will get up in front of the whole church with our pastor and sing songs like "The Anchor Holds." No one will ever accuse him of being the next big thing, but he sings his heart out and doesn't care one bit. I'm not an emotional person. I can usually sit and listen to the greatest singing talent that gospel music has to offer and not shed a tear. But I cry like a baby every time John-John sings. I have never seen John-John when he wasn't smiling, and it humbles me greatly for ever complaining about anything. He is such a blessing, and the Lord uses him greatly. Some people may feel sorry for him. But if John-John could effectively communicate his feelings, they might find out that John-John feels sorry for them.

When I think about these truths, I can't help but think about the Perham family. Brother Ernie and Linda Perham adopted several "special needs" children years ago. Some of their ailments include Down syndrome, spina bifida, and fetal alcohol syndrome. The world didn't give these children a chance, but they travel all over the country, singing and sharing the gospel. Fittingly, one of my favorite songs that they sing is "When others see a shepherd boy, God may see a king." They have blessed my heart in ways that words could never express, and I love all of them dearly. Their selflessness and the way they carry themselves make me want to be a better Christian.

There will always be a special place in my heart for Joshua Perham. His mother was on cocaine while she was pregnant with him. As a result, Joshua was born with a hole in his brain. When the Perhams went to adopt him, the doctors cautioned them, saying that he would never be much more than a vegetable. However, God had different plans. Joshua is now a preacher—and a good one at that. The doctors still don't understand how he is able to function like he does, but I know.

God truly has chosen the foolish things of the world to confound the wise and the weak things of the world to confound the things that are mighty. Just as with John-John and the Perhams, they have a power that men can't teach and money cannot buy. I realized through the truths in God's Word that if the Lord could use the blind, deaf, and dumb, then He wouldn't have any problem using one who had been adopted. He really did have a plan for my life! He has a plan for *every* life. Revelation 4:11 tells us that all things are created for His pleasure. So, if we're not using the gifts He's given us to please Him, then we are flunking out of life.

I never again fretted over the fact that I was adopted. I totally gave it to the Lord, knowing that He was in control. I eventually worked up the courage to ask the principal if I could share my testimony in chapel, and he obliged. I was scared to death. I'm sure that I stumbled and fumbled and made a big mess of things, but I did it just the same. Over the next few months, the Lord opened several doors for me to preach. I preached at several churches throughout West Alabama. I also started going into the juvenile detention center once a week with my youth pastor. If I wasn't preaching, I was there to counsel the inmates during the invitation. There is no greater satisfaction in life than to know that you are doing what God has called you to do.

If there is one purpose that I want this book to serve, it is to show people that God really does have a purpose for every life. He doesn't make mistakes, and there are no accidents with God. A wise person once said, "Has it ever occurred to you that nothing has ever occurred to God?" You were created in His image and for a purpose. I was blessed to find my purpose at a young age. However, there was no way that I could have known how God would specifically use my adoption in the years to follow. I had no clue that He was going to bring things full circle.

9
Through a Mother's Eyes

Lo, children are an heritage of the LORD: and the fruit
of the womb is his reward.
—Psalm 127:3

LIFE WENT ON AS IT ALWAYS does. I graduated from high school
in May of 2003, and a few days later I began classes at the
local community college. After just one semester, I realized that
I was in the wrong place. The Lord was leading me to pursue a
Bible education. I began searching for the right Bible college, which
proved to be rather difficult. I looked at schools from all over the
country. I even visited schools in Georgia and Oklahoma, but I just
couldn't quite feel peace about any of them.

As I prayed and sought the Lord, a friend recommended a great
correspondence program from Gulf Coast Bible Institute out of
Fort Walton Beach, Florida. I checked out the website, tried some
of the courses, and fell in love with it. I enrolled there and got
my education from home. It was one of the best decisions I ever
made. My knowledge of the Bible multiplied a hundredfold. I was
so grateful to have found such sound Bible doctrine.

The months and years after graduation seemed to absolutely
fly by. For the first two and a half years after high school, I was
working part-time and doing my school work in the evenings. But

in October of 2005, I got my first full-time job working night shift at a textile factory that was just a few miles from my house.

Many things stayed the same during this time. I was still living at home. I continued to go to the detention center every week. I was still very close to Brett and Bubba. In fact, Bubba and I worked together at the factory. However, *some* things were changing in front of my eyes. The Lord opened up a door for me to lead the music at Shady Grove Baptist Church, about thirty-five miles north. They didn't have a piano player, but I was able to play the hymns on my guitar. It was a little different, but it worked. It was my first ministry that consistently kept me away from my home church. It was strange being away from Englewood Baptist, the church where I was saved and had been a faithful member for seven years. But I knew this was what the Lord wanted me to do. I greatly enjoyed it and learned a lot in the process.

My routine didn't change much for about the next year. The only real change in my life at all was that I switched to the evening shift at work. But in November of 2006, I hit another milestone. I met the love of my life, Leah Hughes.

I was at a Bible conference at the Unity Baptist Church in Ripley, Mississippi, when I met her. To be totally honest, the first time I saw her I thought she was about twelve years old, even though she was nineteen. She has always looked younger than she really is. I'll never forget the first time we spoke. After the morning service, I was supposed to meet up with some friends to play guitar and sing. I must have carried my guitar around that church five or six times, trying to find my friends, but to no avail. Leah was sitting in the vestibule area at the time.

As I walked by for about the fifth time, she said, "So, can you actually play that guitar, or does it just make you feel important to carry it around?"

I was completely caught off guard. I didn't know if she was being a jerk or if she was trying to flirt or what. That was just Leah, though. She's a big cutup, and I love that about her. We complement each other well, because she keeps me from being such a stick-in-the-mud, and I help to get her serious when needed.

We sat and talked for a while. I found out that she lived in Smithville, Mississippi, where her dad was a pastor. She also told me that she was originally from Tuscaloosa, where I lived, and that most of her family still lived there. After a while, I pulled my guitar out, and we sang some songs together. I knew we had something, right off the bat. We stayed there until it was time to eat supper. But we parted ways, because I was too nervous to sit by her at the meal or at the service that night. I tried to find her after the evening service, but like an idiot, I'd let her get away before I could get her number. I was so mad at myself.

I went back to Tuscaloosa the next morning, feeling extremely distraught. That day when I got back, I immediately got on the Internet to see if I could find her phone number. Surprisingly, it didn't take me very long. I picked up the phone and dialed the number. It rang about three times, and a woman answered the phone: "Hello." I knew it had to be her mother. In a nervous tone, I asked to speak to Leah. "One minute," she said. I could feel my heart begin to race. What would she think about me looking her up? After a few seconds, she came to the phone. "Hello," she said.

"Hey," I said, "do you have any idea who this is?"

"Is this Brandon? Hey, how are you?"

Now if you were to ask Leah what she thought about me calling her that night, she would be quick to tell you that she thought I was some kind of stalker. But the truth is that she was glad I called. We talked for hours, and before we got off the phone, she invited me to the upcoming Bible conference at her church.

The rest is history. We met in November of 2006 and were married on March 19, 2007. Some people might think that's crazy, but when you know, you know. I would do it all over again.

Our first home was located in Coker, Alabama, just a few miles north of Tuscaloosa. One of the first things we did as a newlywed couple was to seek the Lord as to which church He wanted us in. I believe the Lord has a time and a season for everything, and although I loved the people at Englewood, as well as Shady Grove, I felt as if those seasons had come to an end.

We ended up joining Little Sandy Baptist Church, just down the road from where I grew up. I had met the pastor, Brother Ronnie Blake, through the juvenile detention ministry. He and his wife Vicki have been a huge blessing and a great influence on us over the years. I will always claim Brother Ronnie as my pastor.

I think the first year of our marriage would be considered normal. It was filled with a mixture of happiness, ambition, struggles, and adjustment. We were so in love, it was ridiculous. I was working three to eleven in the evenings when we first got married, which worked out great because we were both night owls. I would come home at night, and our day would just be starting. We would go to the Waffle House about midnight and then come home and watch movies or just talk until the wee hours of the morning.

Back while we were dating, I had told Leah about my being adopted. It was kind of just mentioned in passing. Leah couldn't believe that it didn't seem to be a big deal to me that I hadn't met my birth parents and didn't know anything about the past. She would randomly go into these lectures about me needing to search for them. I always just kind of blew it off. The truth is that at that point in my life it was nothing more than a vague curiosity. I was also afraid that the truth might hurt worse than not knowing anything at all. My biological parents might not want anything to do with me, and for all I knew, they could be drug-heads or convicts. The fear always outweighed my curiosity, and I never really had any intention of ever finding them. But all that changed on May 14, 2008.

Leah had found out the previous August that she was pregnant with our first child. Nine grueling months went by. I felt so sorry for Leah. I don't know why someone ever coined the phrase *morning sickness,* because it was more of a twenty-four-hour thing for her. But finally, about three a.m. on May 14th, she was awakened by intense contractions. Not totally sure if it was the real thing, she didn't wake me up until about eight o'clock the next morning, when her water finally broke.

We quickly drove to the Northport Hospital, just minutes away. Leah had pretty much a textbook delivery, and our beautiful son, Wesley, was born about one o'clock that afternoon. I'll never forget the first time I held him. Up to that point, I had never held a baby in my life. I had always been too afraid I might drop it, or it might spit up on me. But you could hardly get our son away from me. I just kept staring at him, looking at his beautiful eyes and smelling his hair. Every person that has ever had the privilege of becoming a parent knows exactly what I'm talking about.

There were so many thoughts running through my mind the day Wesley was born. For one thing, I felt like I learned more about the Lord in the first few minutes of being a father than I had in the past few years. It's impossible for someone to understand the love a parent feels if he has never been one. I couldn't help but think about the love it must have taken for God the Father to give His only begotten Son, Jesus Christ, for a bunch of low-down sinners. I couldn't see giving Wesley up for anyone.

But in the midst of all that happiness, there was a slight dearth that overshadowed me. Of all the things that could have come to my mind at that moment, I couldn't help but think about my birth parents. How could they have given me up? What could drive a person to do such a thing? I was confused, and to be honest, I was kind of angry. But I pushed those feelings aside and soaked up the blessings of the day.

The day continued on, and friends and family were constantly in and out. There were balloons and presents everywhere. It was a special time in our young life. Finally, though, the nighttime came, and things quieted down. It was now just Leah, Wesley, and I in that small hospital room. Leah was understandably exhausted, but sleep seemed to be just a pipe dream at this point. Wesley's body temperature wouldn't stay up, so they had him under the heat lamp on the baby bed next to Leah. The nurses were constantly in and out to check on him, and when they weren't in there, Leah was feeding Wesley. Finally the nurse came in and told Leah that she would be glad to roll the baby down to the nursery so Leah could get some sleep. "Oh, thank you," Leah said. "That would be wonderful."

They rolled him just down the hall to the nursery, and I knew that in a matter of minutes Leah would be out for the count. While she was lying in bed, I was busy posting pictures of the day's events on Facebook, using my laptop. Every now and then I would glance over to see if she had fallen asleep. To my surprise, thirty minutes went by, and every time I looked at her, she was wide-eyed and staring at the ceiling. I finally said, "Babe, are you all right? Why can't you sleep?"

She looked at me and began to cry. "Bring him back," she said. "Bring him back. I can't sleep without knowing for sure that he's okay."

"Well, Babe, he's just two doors down in the nursery," I said.

"I know, but he's supposed to be with me. Please get them to bring him back!"

My common-sense logic was being overpowered by a mother's instinct. She sounded almost desperate, as if we had just given him into the hands of baby brokers. So I walked down the hall and asked the nurse to bring him back into the room.

When the nurse left, Leah asked me to hand Wesley to her. I picked him up out of the baby bed and placed him into her arms. She held him tightly and kissed him as if they had been separated for years. And then it hit me like a ton of bricks! I began to visualize the horror that my birth mother must have gone through when she had to give me up. Surely it couldn't have been something that she wanted to do. She must have felt as if she *had* to.

As I began to analyze everything in front of me, I realized for the first time in my life that giving me up for adoption must have been an act of love. And if that was true, she must have been tormented over it every single day for the past twenty-three years. Something snapped inside of me that night. I had seen my adoption through a mother's eyes. I didn't know exactly how I was going to do it, but I knew one thing for sure: I *had* to find my birth mother!

10
Digging Up Bones

O
UR HOSPITAL STAY LINGERED ON FOR two more days. I didn't tell Leah about my sudden motivation to find my birth mother. We both obviously had a lot on our plate. But the biggest reason that I put it off was because I wanted to make sure that this wasn't just some emotional whim. I knew that if I gave this whole thing some time and thought that it would either go way or get stronger, and as the days went by, it got a *lot* stronger. What's strange is that my desire wasn't so much to find my birth father, but it was very strong to find my mother. Perhaps I figured that since she had carried me for nine months there would automatically be some kind of bond there. It just felt like a safer risk to me.

We had been home from the hospital for a few days, when I finally told Leah of my plans to search for my birth mother. She was elated, as I had known she would be. As the weeks went on, we prayed and asked God to give us wisdom and guidance. I knew that this was going to be a life-changing decision in one way or another, for better or for worse. Since my experience at the hospital, I had made some assumptions, perhaps unfounded, about the past. I assumed that my birth mother had probably been young and unwed when she'd had me and that she hadn't had the means to care for me. By default, I also assumed that if this were true, then there was a good possibility that she had gotten married later in life and had a family. I knew that I could very well have some blood siblings out there somewhere. I had absolutely no proof of any of that, but that is the angle that I chose to take on the situation.

The reason I chose to look at it that way was because it gave me the strength to go through with searching for them. I had been told so many horror stories from other adoptees about finding their birth mothers or fathers and being totally and utterly rejected. Their parents wanted nothing to do with them, and the scary thing was, it seemed that this scenario was the rule rather than the exception. I don't know if it had to do with guilt or what, but it seemed to be prevalent among those who had walked this road that I was about to set out on. If I painted a picture in my mind of a loving mother who wished I would come back into her life, it gave me the courage to proceed, whether it was true or not.

I knew beyond a shadow of a doubt that my only real chance of finding her would be through the adoption agency. A few weeks after we got home from the hospital, I finally got up the nerve to begin the search. June of 2008 was the first time in my life that I ever made any kind of attempt to find my birth mother.

I got on the Internet and located the agency's website, where I obtained the phone number. I picked up the phone, took a deep breath, and dialed the number. It rang a few times, and then a woman picked up. "Caring Hands Services. How may I help you?"

"Yes, ma'am, my name is Brandon Vaughan, and I was adopted through your agency in 1984. I'm trying to find my birth mother, and I was wondering if you could help me."

"Hold on just one second," she said. I could hear the typing of computer keys and knew that she must be looking up my file. "Yes, Mr. Vaughan, I see your information right here."

"So, do you have any information on my mother or father?" I asked.

"I don't have any personal information on your father, but I do have all of your mother's information."

"That's wonderful!" I said. I was overjoyed. This was a lot easier than I'd thought it was going to be. This was just too good to be true. And unfortunately, it was.

Before the lady could reply, I said, "Could you please give me her name and her contact information?" I frantically searched for a pen and something to write on. But it would all be for naught.

"Mr. Vaughan, I'm really sorry, but I can't give you any of that information."

"What? You're telling me that you are staring at my birth mother's information on your computer screen and you can't give it to me?"

"That's what I'm saying," she said in a matter-of-fact tone.

I was dumbfounded. "Well why can't you give it to me?" I asked in utter disbelief.

"Unfortunately, the state of Florida had some incredibly strict and secretive laws in the eighties concerning closed adoption. The truth is that these records are locked for ninety-nine years, and nobody can touch them."

I sat quietly for a few seconds and gathered myself. Within just a few minutes of searching, the mountain that I knew I must climb had gotten a *whole* lot higher. I took a deep breath and went in for round two. "Well if those records are locked for ninety-nine years, then how in the world can I ever hope to find her?"

"You need to get online and check the Florida Reunion Registry. If your birth mother has signed up, you should be able to find her with no problem. But I'm going to be honest with you, Mr. Vaughan. I'm not trying to discourage you, but if she isn't signed up on the registry, then it will be next to impossible to find her."

I felt a pit beginning to form in my stomach. These were neither the words that I had expected or hoped to hear. I thanked her, we bid each other a good-day, and that was that. I immediately went to the computer and pulled up the Florida Reunion Registry. I typed in my birthday and place of birth to see if it matched any of the posts. I must have scrolled down the page for thirty minutes before I accepted the fact that she was nowhere to be found. I then began to wonder what that said about her desire to have any kind of relationship with me. What if she didn't want me in her life? I quickly pushed those thoughts aside and went back to my assumptions.

I was down, but I wasn't out just yet. I was still confident that in the age of social networking and technology I could somehow find her, as I had found Leah a few years earlier. For the next several weeks, I looked at every possible angle by which people could be reunited with their birth parents. I looked at private investigators, nationwide reunion registries, reunion companies, and everything in between. But nothing seemed to get around the fact that those records were off-limits for ninety-nine years. I was beginning to think that my only option was to live to be a hundred, and then at least I could find out what her name was.

As the weeks dragged on, I finally accepted defeat. I had exhausted every resource available to me, and I wasn't any closer than I'd been on the day I started. The door was shut so tightly that I began to think that perhaps it wasn't in God's will or plan for me to find her. Maybe my assumptions were dead wrong, and He was protecting me from something. I was discouraged, but I took solace in the fact that God was in control, and if He'd wanted me to find her, it would have happened.

So I gave up the search, cold turkey. I knew that it was time to move on. I also realized that I was probably going to live my whole life and never know the truth. I had a good life, though, and I could at least find solace in knowing that I had done absolutely all that I could. I could hold my head up high and move on with no regrets.

11
One More Time

Now faith is the substance of things hoped for, the
evidence of things not seen.
—Hebrews 11:1

THE NEXT FOUR YEARS WERE A time of great change in my life. In late 2008, we left Little Sandy to take my first pastorate in the small town of Gordo, Alabama, about twenty-five miles northwest of Tuscaloosa. That same year, Mom and Dad got divorced and moved to separate parts of Tuscaloosa. On January 16, 2010, Leah gave birth to our beautiful baby girl, Allison.

A few months later, I lost my job at the factory, but God opened up another door with a large pest-control company. Within two months on the job, I was able to get a route in the Gordo area. They issued me a company truck, and I only had to commute to the office twice a week. Not only that, but the same day that I was offered the Gordo route, a friend called and asked me if we wanted to buy his late mother's house right there in Gordo. He gave us a great deal, and we moved in within a few months. It's so awesome when we get to see the hand of the Lord working in our lives.

Life didn't seem like it could get any better. I had a good job that gave me the opportunity to work in the area that we had just moved to. We now had two beautiful children, and our house was less than two miles from the church where I was the pastor. The whole adoption ordeal seemed like a distant memory. But it's so amazing how the Lord can change things in an instant.

In the winter of 2011, I remember riding around in my work truck between stops, when it almost seemed like the Lord got into the truck with me. He began once again to put my birth mother heavy upon my heart. The desire to search for her was rekindled in my soul. The only problem was that there was still nothing more that could be done. But the desire to find her was so strong that I actually remember saying out loud, "But I've already tried everything."

It's like the Lord spoke to my heart and said, "Just one more time." There were no other factors in my life at that time to bring her to my mind; it was just the Lord. Even if she didn't want a relationship with me, I had a desire to share with her what the Lord had done in my life and to give her the gospel.

Throughout the day, I racked my brain to try and think of any stone that was left unturned. The only thing I could think of that I hadn't really looked at in the first search were the papers that mom had shown me when I was fifteen. Those papers were nothing but typewriter pages of non-identifying information. I knew it was a long shot, but I thought that perhaps there was some clue that I had overlooked that I might catch, now that I was older.

When I returned home from work, I immediately went to the filing cabinet where I kept important documents. To my surprise, I couldn't find them anywhere. I just *knew* that I had a copy of them in there. I asked Leah if she had moved them, and she said she hadn't.

So I called Mom and asked her if she had a copy. She said, "I'm sure that I do. Hold on a second, and I'll check." It wasn't a strange request to her, because she had known for a long time that I was looking for my birth mother. She was so supportive that I sometimes wondered if she was more excited than I was. A few minutes later, she got back on the phone and said, "Bran, I can't find one anywhere."

I thanked her, and we said good-bye. I was absolutely puzzled. It wasn't uncommon for me to lose something. But Mom kept up with *everything*. I knew the only thing left to do was to call the adoption agency again.

I once again called the adoption agency, as I had done three years earlier. I knew that this was a last-ditch effort. This was the Hail Mary pass down the field on the last play of the game. The phone rang a couple of times before a woman answered the phone: "Caring Hands Services. How may I help you?"

"Hey, this is Brandon Vaughan. I was adopted through your agency in 1984, and I was trying to locate my birth mother. I know that you can't give me any identifying information, but I was wondering if you could mail me the non-identifying information."

"That won't be a problem, Mr. Vaughan. We'll get this in the mail for you," she replied.

That was pretty much it: short, sweet, and to the point. Now I just had to wait and see what happened.

The days turned into weeks, and the weeks turned into months, and the papers never came in the mail. I realized this was probably a sign that I needed to just cut my losses and move on with my life, and that's exactly what I did. I didn't know it at the time, but the storms that were headed our way were about to change my focus anyway.

The year 2011 rolled on, and with it came some fierce trials and tribulations. That was without a doubt the hardest year of my life. The Devil hit my family and me in every way possible. For starters, things began to go downhill fast at the church. I had stretched myself to the limit. On top of working full-time and trying to take care of a wife and two young children, I was teaching Sunday school, leading the singing, preaching three services a week, and doing everything else in between. That was tough enough, but when the church as a whole made it clear that they didn't want us there anymore, it was just too much to bear. It was really taking a toll on me, and it was beginning to show in my family as well. So, in May of that year, I resigned as the pastor.

When we left that church, we went back to our home church at Little Sandy to try and regroup and get our joy back. But the hits just kept on coming. The Devil attacked our finances and tried to attack our marriage and our health. If it hadn't been for the grace of God, we would never have made it through that year. Even if I *had* been able to find my birth mother, I wouldn't have been able to put any effort into building a relationship. Life was just too demanding and difficult. Every storm, however, must come to an end, and the sun will shine again. As 2011 turned into 2012, things really started to turn around.

It had been almost a year since I had called the adoption agency and inquired about mailing the information, and I still hadn't heard from them. However, as providence would have it, that was about to change.

In late January of 2012, I got a phone call out of the blue one day while I was working. When the phone rang, I looked at the number on my caller ID. Not only did I not recognize the number, but it was a different area code. I almost didn't answer, thinking that it was a telemarketer, but my curiosity got the best of me. I answered the phone: "Hello."

"Hello, Mr. Vaughan. This is Amy with Caring Hands Services. How are you today?"

"I'm good," I said, trying to hide my surprise.

"Mr. Vaughan, we were doing some cleaning around the office, and I found that your file had fallen behind one of the filing cabinets. I see a note on it that says we were supposed to mail your birth mother's non-identifying information to you. I'm so sorry about this mix-up. We will get this in the mail today."

I thanked her for her concern, and we struck up a conversation about the adoption, as well as my failed search. Amy was different from the other ladies that I had spoken with. She seemed to really want to help me. We talked for about twenty minutes before getting off the phone, and I just had a good feeling about everything. Perhaps the Hail Mary had found an open receiver in the end zone after all.

As long as I live, I will never forget what happened just a few days later. It was a Sunday evening, and we had just returned home from church. Just before we pulled into the driveway, I stopped by the mailbox to retrieve the mail. We had been out of town that weekend, so we hadn't been able to check it. We unloaded the car, went into the house, and changed into our bed clothes. I sat down on our bed, and as I looked through the stack of mail, I noticed that I had a package from the adoption agency.

I opened the envelope, expecting to see the same typed copies of information that I had seen previously. But what I saw blew me away. Instead of a typed copy, it was a copy of the actual, handwritten information from 1984. It had all of my birth mother's information, as well as her family's information. However, the information that I wasn't supposed to see was blacked out with a permanent marker. I felt a cold chill run up my spine, and my face obviously showed my astonishment, as Leah said, "What is it, Brandon? What is it?" I was speechless as I held it up for her to see. I knew, without even taking a closer look, that I was holding in my hand the smoking gun that would solve the mystery of my past.

I have always wondered if Amy did it on purpose to help me, and I guess I'll never know. The truth is that she probably could just as easily have sent a copy with the identifying information left blank. But having said that, the information was blacked out extremely well.

I stared at that paper so hard that I thought I was going to burst a blood vessel, but I couldn't make out anything. I held it up to the light, front-ways and back, to see if anything would show through, but to no avail. I was beginning to wonder if I had once again gotten my hopes up for nothing. I ran to the dresser drawer and pulled out a flashlight. To my astonishment, I found that if I turned off the bedroom light and held the flashlight at just the right angle I could make out a few words.

Feeling like a forensic detective, I began to carefully examine my birth mother's information. I started with the name. I could make out that her first name was Cheryl! I was already almost in tears at this point, just knowing her first name after all these years. The rest of her name was blacked out too well to see. I guess that would have just been too easy. I diligently went down the page, trying to uncover any more useful information. However, the only other information that I was able to make out was that she had graduated in 1983 and that she'd had a Florida address at the time. That meant that she would have been eighteen or nineteen at the time she gave birth to me, depending on when her birthday fell. She must be about forty-seven now. I was elated at finding this evidence, but it still wasn't enough.

I began to flip through the other pages of information on her closest family members. I couldn't make out much of anything, but on page three I finally hit the jackpot. I could see very clearly that one of her brothers was named Douglas Heath and that he had been twenty-two years old at the time I was born. That meant that he would be about forty-nine now.

I now knew that, in all likelihood, I was looking for a Cheryl Heath, around the age of forty-seven, who had had a Florida address in 1984. I figured that she most likely had gotten married at some point in the past twenty-seven years, and in that case, her name would have changed. My best chance was to find her brother Douglas and then trace her through him, because his name would have stayed the same.

Leah and I were absolutely on cloud nine. There was no doubt that the Lord was up to something. Unfortunately, we would have to wait until the next day to resume our search, because we didn't have Internet access at our house at the time, and it was too late to go anywhere. Needless to say, it was one of the longest nights of my life, not to mention the next day at work. I knew beyond a shadow of a doubt that with the information I had acquired it was finally going to happen. I was finally going to find my birth mother!

It seemed like an eternity, but I finally got off work that following Monday morning. The second I got off, I went to meet Leah at Mom's house so we could get on the Internet. I went to a people-search website and searched the entire United States for a Douglas Heath. There were over sixty hits, and I couldn't believe that the one at the very top of the list was forty-nine and was listed as having a sister named Cheryl! His current address was in Ohio, but it showed that he had previously lived in Florida. I cross-referenced his sister, Cheryl. It said that her last name was Culpepper, that she was forty-seven, and that she lived in Winter Haven, Florida. I knew this *had* to be it!

I paid thirty dollars to do a complete background check on Cheryl Culpepper. The background check brought up fourteen pages of information on her. But the one thing that I really wanted to see was at the very top of page one. In big, bold letters, it said: "Maiden Name: Cheryl Heath." I don't really know if I can effectively communicate how I felt at that moment when all doubt was removed. I felt a sense of relief and victory. But I also couldn't help but feel like I was a part of something so much bigger than myself, something divine. There were so many circumstances that had had to come together just right for me to have found her. I got so caught up in the moment that I almost forgot that my work wasn't finished yet.

I began to scan down the small novel of information. It would scare you to death to know what someone can find out about you for just thirty dollars. I circled the important stuff: address, phone number, etc. But then, to my amazement, I came to the page containing her closest relatives. It was there that I saw the names of my siblings: Devin, Forrest, and Amber. I was so full of emotion, I just don't even know how to describe it. I was so happy, but at the same time, I was filled with so many questions. Did they know about me? Did they want me in their lives? I wondered what they were like.

I finished scanning through all the pages of information, and then I immediately got on Facebook. Surely at least one of them would have an account. I looked up my birth mother but found nothing. However, when I looked up Amber's name, there she was. I scrolled through all of her pictures until I came across one of what appeared to be her high school graduation. Amber was standing on the football field, wearing a white gown and yellow sash. Standing to her right were Forrest and Devin, and to her left was my birth mother. Seeing her face for the first time left no doubt that I was hers. She couldn't have denied me if she'd wanted to, for we favored each other heavily. Forrest favored me greatly as well. He looked so much like me, in fact, that when I later showed that same picture to my pastor, he thought it was me. I can't accurately describe what I was feeling when, for the first time in my life, I was staring at my blood kin. The greatest quotes from the most elegant poets could never have sufficed. Having never even met them, I had such a love in my heart for all of them. It's a strange thing to love someone that you've never even met, but that's exactly what I felt as I gazed at their picture on Facebook that day.

Now came the critical issue. How should I go about contacting them? I realized that it must be handled delicately. I didn't know if my siblings—or even her husband—knew about me, and I didn't want to cause a problem in her family for something that happened so long ago. I knew that, whatever I did, I had to speak directly to her. I had a friend who had been adopted from birth. She, like me, had found her birth mother, but sadly hers was one of those horror stories where her mother didn't want anything to do with her. She had given me some great advice for the day I ever decided to contact my birth parents. She said the best thing I could do was to use a mediator to call them. By doing this, it would save them the total shock of hearing their long lost child on the other end of the phone, but it would also save me some of the hurt if they should reject me. So that is exactly what I did.

Leah was more than willing to do it, and I trusted her completely. I tried to give her somewhat of a script. There were three things that I wanted to accomplish: first of all, to make sure that my birth mother was the one on the phone; second, to find out if she had given up a son up for adoption in 1984; and last, to find out if she wanted any kind of relationship with me. We went over it a couple of times, and then it was time.

I walked into the next room. I couldn't bear to listen to what was being said. I paced around like an expectant father for only a few minutes before Leah came into the room. "All of the numbers we have are no longer in service," she said with a disappointed look. I couldn't help but laugh out loud. We had done the impossible to get this far, and now, of all things, we couldn't get an updated phone number. They must have done like so many others and gotten rid of their lan line when cell phones became so affordable.

It was getting late, so we decided to head back home and try our luck again tomorrow. The following day while I was at work, Leah tried in vain to find an updated number. There's just not a great way to look up cell phone numbers. Tuesday's results yielded nothing.

On Wednesday, we decided to go to plan B. I really didn't want to have to go through a middleman, but I realized at this point that it was a necessary evil. The background report gave us a list of her fourteen closest relatives with all of their contact information, as well as their fourteen closest neighbors and all of their contact information. Leah and I agreed that she would go down the list and try to get my birth mom's phone number while I was at work. The plan was that she would, under no circumstances, tell anyone who we were and why we were calling. All day long she called neighbors and relatives, trying to get my birth mother's phone number. Most of those numbers were disconnected as well, and the people that she *was* able to get on the phone didn't want to give out her information without knowing why we were calling. Wednesday also yielded no results. However, on Thursday we finally hit pay dirt.

12
For This My Son Was Dead, And Is Alive Again

February 2, 2012
Cheryl's Perspective

I was suddenly awakened out of a deep sleep by my alarm clock. I rubbed my eyes and rolled over to see that Ronnie had already gotten up. It wasn't unusual for him to get up early and head to the office. A few days had now come and gone since my birthday, as well as my night of remorse. Over the past twenty-seven years, I had definitely had my fair share of moments concerning the past, but they had all come and gone in a somewhat reasonable fashion. However, this time it had been different. I just couldn't shake it off as easily as I had so many times before. Don't get me wrong. Giving up my son wasn't something that controlled my life. It was just something that nagged at me all the time. I had really hoped that he would have found me by now. However, the truth was that I didn't even know if my son was dead or alive.

I began for the first time ever to question my decision about not searching for my son. I knew that I had done the right thing by leaving him and his family alone when he was younger, but he was an adult now. He probably even had a family of his own by this time. I just kept wondering whether or not he knew that he had been adopted. Had anyone ever told him? Didn't I have some kind of moral obligation to at least tell him what had happened? I had so many questions racing through my mind. *Should* I set out in search of my son?

I just dismissed the idea as a ridiculous fantasy, as I wiped the sleep from my eyes. For all these years, my son had been dead to me, and I knew that, no matter how much it ate at me, he probably wasn't coming back today or any other day. Maybe I just needed to stop getting my hopes up. Then I wouldn't have to deal with the disappointment.

I forced myself to get out of bed and start my day, and after a shower and a change of clothes, I was feeling a little better. I went into the kitchen to start cooking breakfast. I'm not much of a breakfast person, but Mom was staying with us, and I knew she needed something to eat. Her health had taken a turn for the worse right around Thanksgiving, so we were looking after her. It really killed me to see her go down like that. Mom and I had definitely had some bumps in the road when it came to our relationship, but in recent years, we had gotten a lot closer. I made sure that she was taken care of, and then I headed out the door to the office.

Ronnie and I own a partnership in our family trucking company. We run about twenty-five trucks all over the south. It's a little stressful, to say the least, but at least work could get my mind off the past. I walked into the office and took my usual place at my desk. It was Thursday, and that meant that payroll had to be done. It was going to be a long day.

There was very little idle time, and as a result, the hours seemed to fly by. I left the office around four p.m. to go home and start cooking supper. It seemed to be just another typical day in the life of Cheryl Culpepper. After we'd eaten supper and the dishes were washed, I changed into my bed clothes and settled in for the night. As I walked into the living room, I saw that Mom was seated on the couch, watching baseball reruns on the MLB network. I never understood why a woman her age would be so consumed by baseball, but she never missed a game, especially if the Braves were playing. I took a seat in the recliner, and we struck up a conversation full of small talk.

Ronnie was next door at his sister Sherry's house. There was hardly a day that went by that he didn't go over there for at least a little while. I think he got tired of fighting with Mom for control of the TV. He had been over there for about an hour or so, when I heard the kitchen door open. Ronnie peaked around the kitchen door so Mom wouldn't see him. He quietly motioned for me to come outside. So I casually got up like I was going to the kitchen and followed him out the side door. Ronnie is kind of a drama queen, so I couldn't help but wonder what had happened *this* time.

As soon as we got outside, I said, "Ronnie, what's wrong?"

"Something strange is going on," he said with a rare and serious tone in his voice.

I was all ears now. "What do you mean?" I asked.

"Well earlier today a young woman called my mother asking for your phone number. The woman wouldn't give any information or reason for calling, so Mom didn't give her your number.

"So, what's the big deal about that?" I asked.

"That's not all," he replied. "When I came over to Sherry's house, the first thing she said to me was that a young woman had also called *her*, trying to get ahold of you. The young lady wouldn't tell Sherry anything either. So I called the number back and talked to her myself. She swore she wasn't a bill collector or anything, but she wouldn't tell me who she was or why she was trying to get in touch with you. I said that I would get you to call her back if she would just give me some kind of a hint to tell you. She told me that it was a private family matter. We looked up the area code, and it's an Alabama number. We have no idea who it could be or what it could be about. But Cheryl, I've just got a feeling."

"A feeling about what," I asked in an anxious tone.

"I think this may be the call."

"The call? What call?" I asked.

"The call that you have been waiting for since 1984," he said with a childlike excitement in his voice.

I felt my heart jump into my throat. Ronnie's a practical joker, but he would never have said something like this if he didn't really believe it. "You're scaring me, Ronnie. Don't do this."

"No, Cheryl, I'm telling you this is it. I think your son has found you, and this girl is some kind of a mediator. All I want to know is, do you want me to call the number back?"

Without even thinking about it, I said, "Sure," although I was now scared to death. For all the time I'd fantasized about my son making his return into my life, I had never actually thought about what to do or what to say if it actually happened. I felt like I was about to take a big exam that I hadn't studied for.

Ronnie pulled out his phone and called the number. I was so nervous that I felt as if I was going to be sick. I walked back inside the house. It was just too much to process. I paced back and forth in the kitchen like a caged lion. After only a few seconds, Ronnie came back inside. "No answer," he said. "I'll call back in a few minutes." The suspense was almost more than I could handle. I went back into the living room so Mom wouldn't get suspicious.

I sat back down in the recliner and tried to keep my overwhelming emotion in check. I attempted to watch the ball game with Mom, but it was pointless. I was now hopelessly in dreamer mode. I kept reminding myself that it could be absolutely nothing. A young, anonymous woman searching for me was definitely strange, but at that point, that was all it was: strange. Ronnie just seemed so convinced, though. I didn't know if I had ever seen him act quite like this. I sat there for what seemed like hours, but in reality it was probably only twenty minutes later when Ronnie reappeared in the kitchen and once again motioned for me to come outside.

I got up and walked outside to see what the verdict was. Ronnie was waiting for me by the car in the driveway. "I'm about to call back. I just wanted you to be here when I do," he said. He took a deep breath, hit redial, and put the phone to his ear. After a few seconds, someone on the other end must have picked up, for Ronnie jumped and said, "Hello, this is Ronnie Culpepper, Cheryl's husband. I just wanted to get back with you and ask you a few questions, if that's okay. Look, I know that you don't want to tell me what this is about, but I've just got a feeling that this has to do with something that happened a long time ago. Does this have something to do with 1984?"

All of a sudden, Ronnie's eyes got as big around as saucers. He looked up at me, held his hand up in the air, and gave me the nod. My dream had finally come true! This was the moment that I had waited twenty-seven years for, and now that it was here, I didn't know what to do.

I know it sounds crazy, but as soon as Ronnie confirmed that it was my son who was looking for me, I went back inside and sat down with Mom in the living room. I was so nervous. I now knew that it was my son, but I didn't know why he was calling. Was he angry? Did he hate me? There was no accurate way to explain how I was feeling. I was relieved, overjoyed, worried, nervous, and confused—all at the same time. As Ronnie was outside on the phone, I sat there in the living room in an absolute state of euphoria.

To make things even more interesting, Mom looked up at me in the middle of all this and said, "What's wrong, Cheryl? What's going on?" I was completely caught off guard by the question. Was I so naïve to think that she wouldn't notice that something unusual was going on? I began to wonder what Mom's reaction would be if she knew that my son had found me. What would she think after all these years? I mean, she *was* the governing factor over the whole adoption. Through the years, the adoption had absolutely been a taboo subject. We just didn't talk about it. However, I thought that she deserved to know, so I told her the truth.

"Mom, my son has found me, and Ronnie is outside on the phone with a young woman that we believe is acting as his mediator.

That's all I know right now." All of a sudden her countenance completely changed. I saw the tears of twenty-seven years of regret begin to well up in her eyes. She took a moment to gather herself and then said, "Good, maybe I will get to see him again before I die." And with that, she got up and headed to her bedroom for the night. She never did like for other people to see her emotional, but it was too late. I had seen a side of my mother that I had never seen before. I was so relieved that she was happy about the possibility of a reunion.

I sat there in the living room by myself, trying to process everything. I was convinced that my son was going to have at least some kind of anger and resentment toward me. But I felt like whatever it was, it could be worked out. The bottom line was that I was finally going to get some answers. I was finally going to get to bury the past. I was finally going to see my son! All of a sudden, I was jolted from my thoughts by the sound of the kitchen door opening. *Here we go,* I thought to myself.

Brandon's Perspective

I was anxiously pacing back and forth in the freezing cold, while Leah was on the phone with my birth mom's husband, Ronnie. For the past two days, Leah had tried to get her phone number from her relatives and hadn't had any luck. Ronnie had called Leah back earlier that day, and after talking to her for a while, had told her that Cheryl would call her back. Even though we were anxiously awaiting the call, I had committed to preach at the Juvenile Detention Center that night. As was the custom, I went in with the guys, and Leah went in with the girls. We weren't allowed to have our phones in the prison, so, needless to say, it was harder than usual to stay focused on my sermon.

As soon as we were finished, we walked to the car and checked Leah's phone. We noticed that Ronnie had called while we were inside, and just as Leah was about to call him back, her phone rang. It was Ronnie. I left Leah in the car to talk to him, and I paced back and forth in the parking lot. It was a cold February night, and I didn't even have a jacket with me. However, I couldn't bear the thought of listening in on the conversation. I just knew that they had figured out why we were calling and that Ronnie was calling to tell us that they wanted to leave the past in the past: thank you, and have a nice life. In a humorous way, I felt as if I was back in middle school and had just gotten one of my friends to ask a girl out for me and was awaiting the verdict. I was so scared of rejection. I couldn't think of anything worse than my own mother not wanting to have anything to do with me. I had paced around in the cold for about twenty minutes, when I saw Leah hang up the phone and motion for me to get into the car. *Here we go*, I thought to myself.

I got back into the car and cranked up the heater. I looked over at Leah and said, "So, hit me with it. What's the story?"

"Well Ronnie figured it out," she said, "and he's known about the adoption since before they were married. And I've got some great news. Your birth mom is very happy that you found her! Ronnie said that she definitely wants to try and build a relationship with you."

I was so relieved and happy to hear those words. My birth mom really did love me after all. I didn't realize exactly how much that meant to me, until I was afraid that I would be rejected. The conversation after that was just kind of clouded with details. I had already heard the words that I so desperately wanted to hear.

Cheryl's Perspective

Ronnie walked in the kitchen door, sat down on the couch, and jumped right into the conversation. "All right, here's the deal. First of all, you'll be glad to know that he's not mad or bitter at all. He wants to get to know you, and if possible, establish a relationship with all of us." With those words, I felt an overwhelming wave of relief flow over me. I was zoned in as Ronnie continued on. "The woman on the phone is his wife, Leah, and get this: you're a grandmother! He has a three-year-old son, Wesley, and a two-year-old daughter, Allison." I was beginning to wonder what I had done to deserve such incredible, life-changing news. There's no amount of money that could have bought a moment like I experienced that night.

Before Ronnie could say another word, I cut in with the million-dollar question: "What's his name?"

"His name is Brandon Vaughan. He grew up—and still lives—in the Tuscaloosa, Alabama, area. He's got a job with a pest control company. And check this out: he's a Baptist preacher. In fact, Leah scared me to death when she picked up the phone, because she apologized to me for missing my call because they were "in Juvenile." I thought we had really gotten ourselves into a mess when she said that. But she went on to explain that they are involved with a prison ministry." Ronnie and I burst into laughter. Leave it to Ronnie to break the mood.

As I listened to Ronnie describe Brandon to me, it sounded like he was a pretty stand-up guy. But the truth is that he could have been a fugitive on the run from justice and I would have loved him just the same. I love all four of my children the same, even though one of them I had never even met or spoken with.

Ronnie and I sat there in the living room, rehearsing all of the night's events. A sudden joy filled our house that we hadn't felt in a long time. I kept pinching myself to make sure that I wasn't dreaming. It just seemed too good to be true. We began discussing the next phase of this process, because we knew that this was going to be life-changing for everyone involved. Ronnie and Leah had agreed to mediate until Brandon and I were ready to talk, which I thought was a great idea. I had already made up my mind that I wasn't going to talk to Brandon until I had sat down with the kids and told them about their brother and the events of the past. I just felt like that was the right thing to do. Although I was a little nervous, I knew that they would take it well. They are very accepting, wonderful people. Now I just had to come up with the right time and the right way in which to tell them.

It was getting really late, and there was nothing left to be done for the night, so Ronnie and I headed to bed. As I was lying there in bed, I felt as if the weight of the world had been lifted off my shoulders. There was no more guessing, no more nagging questions, and no more worry. I closed my eyes and drifted off into the most peaceful sleep that I had experienced in almost thirty years.

13
A Family Secret

Cheryl's Perspective

I felt like a little girl on Christmas day when I awoke the next morning. In many ways, it seemed as if I was starting a whole new life. I went through my usual morning routine with an unusual pep in my step, before heading out to the office.

As I walked through the front door of the office, it was incredibly obvious that Ronnie had spilled the beans to all of the employees. I had office staff, truck drivers, vendors, and everyone in between coming up to me and hugging my neck, congratulating me on the wonderful news. It was a miracle that Ronnie had held on to this secret for all of these years, and I believe he would have exploded if he'd had to wait any longer. I didn't mind, though. The reception I got from the employees was extremely heartwarming. It was also a solemn reminder of just how big and how special this was. It just seemed to touch everyone so deeply. I guess it's not every day that your long lost son returns after more than quarter of a century. I felt as if I was living in a Hallmark movie.

I knew, however, that it was only a matter of time before word got back to the kids. Winter Haven is a small town and news travels quickly. I had to come up with a plan, and fast. I figured that the worst possible thing that could happen would be for the kids to find out about their brother from someone other than me. I simply couldn't let that happen. I would have liked for everyone to get together that very day so I could lay it all out on the table. But I knew that it would be impossible with all of their different work and college schedules. At least tomorrow was Saturday, and everyone would be off then.

The first thing I did when I got settled in my office was send them a text message. I simply told them all to meet up at Friday's restaurant in Orlando the next day at six p.m. and that we had some very important family business to discuss. Although I know that they were all curious, the boys simply responded with "okay." Amber, on the other hand, was a nervous wreck. She called me back the very first chance she got and asked what was going on. I told her that everything was okay but that we were going to wait until everyone was together to talk about it. Amber just couldn't understand why I couldn't tell her right then, and I didn't blame her.

It's amusing to look back at it now, as Amber kept prying for answers. "You and Ronnie aren't getting a divorce, are you?" she asked.

"No," I said with a smile.

"Mom, you're not pregnant, are you?"

I burst into laughter and said, "No, sweetheart, those days are long gone." I sure wasn't pregnant, but a child *was* coming into the family. So she wasn't as off-the-mark as she might have thought. I reassured her that everything was okay and that we would discuss it over dinner the following day. She reluctantly agreed, and we said our good-byes before hanging up the phone.

After I got that out of the way, I began to make a feeble attempt at getting my work done. It was an almost impossible task, under the circumstances. I was almost giddy as I sat there at my desk, mulling over the small mountain of paperwork. I had been at work for a few hours, when Ronnie walked in and said, "Let me get on the computer. I've got something that you're going to want to see."

He definitely had me curious, so I rolled my chair out of the way and let him have the computer. As I watched him pull up his e-mail account, he said to me, "Leah just sent me a text message, saying that she e-mailed me some pictures of her and Brandon and the kids." My heart began to race at the thought of seeing my son and his family. For all of these years, I had wondered what he looked like. I had always wanted to know if he had any of my facial features, and within a matter of seconds, I was going to find out.

Finally, Ronnie uploaded the pictures onto the monitor, and there he was, my son. He was sitting on a log, wearing blue jeans and a khaki jacket. There was a river behind him, and on the far side you could see that the leaves were changing colors with the arrival of fall. He had a sincerely happy smile on his face. It was like something pulled straight out of a dream. He had my eyes, my straight hair, and my smile. There was no doubt that he was mine. Ronnie said, "Look at that, Cheryl. He looks just like you!"

I immediately felt the mixed tears of happiness and regret begin to roll down my face. I'm not sure if I can accurately verbalize what I was feeling at that moment. It's so strange to wonder about something for so long and then to finally have your questions answered. I had always pictured him in my imagination, and now, there he was before my eyes. Through the years I had also worried about whether or not he was happy, and seeing his smile answered that question as well. To have those blanks filled in was a special feeling that I will always remember.

After staring for the longest time, I began to scroll down through the rest of the pictures. The next one was a picture of Brandon and Leah together. They were standing side by side in what appeared to be a living room. Leah looked beautiful in her a black-and-yellow striped sweater, and Brandon had on a blue, button-up shirt. They looked so happy together.

The next two pictures were of the grandkids. Wesley was standing in front of a church in a Sunday suit and tie. He was holding a Bible under his arm like a little preacher man. He had blonde hair and the prettiest blue eyes. Then there was Allison, decked out in a

Sunday dress, with her sandy brown hair and beautiful smile. They were like angels. I was overwhelmed with joy. I was so glad that, although I had missed all of those early memories with Brandon, at least there would be some consolation in being able to share the future with them.

I was completely worthless for the rest of the day. I would have accomplished just as much sitting at home. I just kept staring at that first picture of Brandon. I must have said to myself a hundred times that day, "I can't believe it's really him. I *can't believe* it's really him!" Saturday night just couldn't come fast enough. I was ready to talk to him, to explain the past, and to catch up on the past twenty-seven years.

Brandon's Perspective

The next day seemed to drag on. After finally making contact the night before, work was the furthest thing from my mind. I anxiously pondered what the next step would be. Ronnie had mentioned to Leah that they would probably want to tell the kids before we did anything else, which made perfect sense to me. I just wondered when that would be and what would happen after that.

Not long before my last stop of the day, Leah sent me a text message to let me know that Ronnie wanted to talk to me and that he would be calling me within the next few minutes. I was both nervous and excited. What would it be like to talk to the man that had been married to my birth mom for almost twenty years?

Not even two minutes after I got Leah's text, my phone rang. I looked down to see that it was an 863 area code, so I knew it had to be Ronnie. I immediately pulled my work truck over and answered the phone. "Hello," I said nervously.

"Is this Brandon?" Ronnie asked.

"It's me," I replied. Ronnie than began to open up the conversation, which was good, because I really didn't know what to say. "It's so good to hear your voice, Brandon. I just want you to know that your mom is so relieved that you finally found her. There has been a huge weight lifted off her shoulders, because she has been burdened with guilt and worry about the adoption ever since it happened."

"That's good to know," I said, "because I was really worried about what her reaction would be."

"Well she definitely wants to establish a relationship with you, and that's what I'm calling about. I know that you have to be wondering what's happening on our end, so I just called to give you an update. The plans are to get together with the kids in Orlando tomorrow at 6:00 p.m. She is going to sit down with them and tell them all about the situation. After that, she plans on calling you." I was so excited to hear that news! Now I had a time line.

My excitement, however, was quickly invaded by fear. What would the kids think about all of this? They had no idea that I was even in the world. Would they feel like I was infringing upon their lives? I asked Ronnie this very question, and he assured me that although they would be shocked; they would be fine with it. I had no choice but to take him at his word. Besides, we had come too far to turn back now.

Ronnie and I talked for about another twenty minutes or so before we got off the phone. We rehearsed some of the details of this incredible event in our lives. We also talked about general stuff, favorite football teams, hobbies, and so on. Just before we got off the phone, Ronnie said he would keep me updated over the next twenty-four hours and that I had nothing to worry about. I thanked him, and we said our good-byes as we hung up. Ronnie was extremely easy to talk to, and I was glad, because there was really nothing to prepare me for how to execute all of this. I was just ready to get this show on the road. I was ready for Saturday night.

Cheryl's Perspective

Friday had come and gone, and Saturday finally arrived. I woke up that morning with butterflies in my stomach. There was so much on my mind. In just a matter of hours, I was going to look my children in the eye and reveal to them this secret that I had carried for so long. They are wonderful people, and I knew deep down that they would take it like mature adults. But there was still a lingering fear. I mean, this was a *huge* deal. I knew that I couldn't slide by with a simple, "Oh, by the way, you have an older brother that I never told you about, and he wants to come into our lives." I was worried that they might think less of me for all the decisions I'd made twenty-seven years ago. I was even more afraid of them being angry that I had never told them, and I wouldn't blame them. Perhaps I should have told them, but all of that was beside the point now.

To add to my mental circus, I knew that, shortly after the family talk, I was going to get to speak to my son for the first time ever! It was an unstable combination of good and bad stress, to say the least. So I kept myself busy to pass the time. I did some chores around the house and ran some errands. I also went to Mom's house to tidy up a bit. The minutes seemed like hours, and the hours seemed like days, but at last the time finally came.

The drive to Orlando from our house is about forty minutes, so at a quarter after five we loaded up in Devin's car and headed out to meet Forrest and Amber. Ronnie and Devin rode up front, and I sat in the backseat with my thoughts. They kept a pretty steady stream of small talk going up front as we made our way up the interstate, but there was definitely a growing tension in the air. Ronnie was doing his best to hide it, but it was obvious that he was on edge. Meanwhile, I kept rehearsing in my mind what I wanted to say, as I watched the sun disappear into the Florida sky.

When we arrived at Friday's, Amber was there waiting for us. Forrest was running a little behind, as usual. That boy never gets in a hurry about anything. We had already sat down in a corner booth and ordered our drinks, when Forrest walked in. We sat there looking at the menus and chit-chatting, just like we would normally do at a family meal. But it was clear that everyone was nervous.

Everybody was trying so hard not to be awkward, which just seem to add to the awkwardness.

We ordered our food, and the waiter took our menus. It was now time to get this over with. I spoke up and said, "Look, I know that you're all wondering what all this is about, so I'll just jump right into it." I took a deep breath and proceeded. "Do you remember when I told you guys that I acted out and made some really irresponsible decisions as a teenager?" They all shook their heads in reply. I could already feel the emotions taking over, as the tears began to flow. I had promised myself that I wouldn't cry, but it was a foregone conclusion now. Nonetheless, I had to continue. "Well, when I was nineteen, I got pregnant, and I gave my son up for adoption. Two days ago, he contacted us, and he wants to try and build a relationship with all of us. Ronnie has talked to him, but I haven't yet. I wanted to tell you guys about everything and get your input first, because I just felt like it was the right thing to do."

They sat there in silence with stunned looks on their faces for a few seconds, and then Devin finally broke the silence. "Well why didn't you keep him?" he asked. I then began to explain why I couldn't take care of him. I told them the whole story, from the time that I found out I was pregnant, to my mom arranging the closed adoption, to the day that he was born—and how I hadn't heard anything since.

After I had gone through the whole scenario, Forrest spoke up in an agitated tone. "I just don't understand why things were handled that way. It just kind of feels like a family member was betrayed." The others shook their heads in agreement. I told them that, although it was extremely painful and difficult, I had always felt like it was the right thing to do, that it was the best thing I could have done for their brother. That seemed to calm them somewhat.

I watched Amber in the corner trying to hold back the tears. She had remained silent the whole time we were conversing. However, when the waiter brought out our food and headed back to the kitchen, she looked up with a smirk on her face and said,

"Well, Devin, it looks like you've been demoted. You're not the oldest anymore." We all broke out into laughter. It was a wonderful release from the seriousness of the mood. It was also proof that they had taken the news like I knew that they would: like caring, mature adults.

For the next hour we talked about all of the different phases of this life-changing scenario. Ronnie and I told them everything we knew about their brother—that his name was Brandon Vaughan, that he had grown up in Tuscaloosa, Alabama, and that he was a Baptist preacher. We also told them that he was married and had two children. I think they were all excited about having a niece and nephew.

As the family sat there talking, one thing became crystal clear: we were all on the same page. It was obvious that they had love and concern for the brother they had never met. The conversation had started out with a painful past, but now talk had completely shifted to a hopeful future. There was an air of excitement as we entertained plans for a reunion. A massive weight was lifted off my shoulders, now that I had finally unveiled this family secret. The biggest dream of my life was to see all four of my children together and happy, and now it seemed like a real possibility.

After we finished talking, we paid the bill and walked outside. Just before we said our good-byes and headed our separate ways, Ronnie spoke up and said, "Before y'all go, let's take a family picture and text it to Brandon." So the kids and I stood arm-in-arm with a smile, as Ronnie took a picture with his phone. I thought it was a great gesture, knowing that Brandon was probably nervous about how our meeting had gone.

We all hugged and said our good-byes before going our separate ways. Ronnie, Devin, and I loaded into the car. Ronnie sat in the front seat, texting Brandon before he put the car in drive. A few minutes after we got onto the highway, Ronnie pulled out his phone and attempted to hand it to me. "Go ahead and call him," he said, trying to keep a straight face. I quickly pushed his hand back. He knew good and well that I wasn't about to make this all-important phone call with a gawking audience present. "Well I'm going to go ahead and call him so I can update him on everything," he said as he began to dial the number.

Brandon's Perspective

I sat there in my living room with the TV on, looking at the clock every few minutes. I was as nervous as a long-tailed cat in a room full of rocking chairs, knowing that the family discussion was taking place. I was almost sick to my stomach in fear over what the siblings would think about me coming into their lives. I mean, as shocking as it was for Ronnie and my birth mom to get Leah's call, they at least had *some* awareness that it could happen someday. This was probably going to be the most mind-blowing news the siblings had ever received. I just didn't want them to feel like I was infringing upon their life.

The clock read 6:27 p.m. They had now been at the restaurant for almost an hour and a half. They *had* to be getting out soon. I was about to go crazy! Thankfully, it was only a few minutes later that I got a text message from Ronnie. I opened it up to see a picture of my birth mom and all the siblings, smiling, arm-in-arm. It seemed to be their way of letting me know that everything was okay. Although I was still concerned that they might be putting up a front just to keep the peace, the kind gesture did help to ease my tension.

A few minutes after the text, Ronnie called me. I answered, "Hello."

"Hey, Brandon, it's Ronnie. I was just calling to let you know that we're out of the restaurant and that everything went well. The kids were obviously shocked and had some questions, but they are good with everything."

"That's great," I replied, "because I care a lot about what they think about this whole thing."

"Well everything is good. You have nothing to worry about. I was just calling to give you an update and to let you know that your mom is probably going to call you within the next thirty minutes or so."

"Sounds good," I replied, trying to hide my nerves. We said our good-byes and hung up the phone.

I looked over at Leah, who was seated on the couch, and said in a shaky tone, "She's going to call in about thirty minutes or so."

"Well, I'm sure after getting this far, you have nothing to worry about," she replied. "This is all just so amazing." I was thankful for her support, but I *had* to be alone. I told her that I needed some privacy and headed to our bedroom, shutting the door behind me. I laid my phone on the dresser and sat down in the recliner. All I could do now was wait.

14
Long-Distance Call

Cheryl's Perspective

We finally pulled into our driveway after what seemed to be an unusually long drive back from Orlando. We all got out of the car and headed into the house. As soon as I'd put my leftovers into the refrigerator, I asked Ronnie to give me his phone. He already had Brandon's number saved, so it would be one less thing I had to worry about. He gave me an amused smile as he handed me the phone, because he knew that I was about to explode from all of the different emotions I was feeling.

I took the phone and walked outside to my quiet place on our front porch. It's just a little slab of concrete under an awning, furnished with a couple of wicker chairs, but it's where I like to get away. It was certainly a fitting place for this all-important phone call. As I sat there for a minute, gathering myself, I looked over to my left and saw Ronnie peeking his head around the corner of the house. "What are you doing?" I asked.

He laughed and said, "I couldn't help myself. I just wanted to see the look on your face the first time you hear his voice."

I just snickered and rolled my eyes. You just have to know Ronnie. "I'll tell you all about it when I'm done, but you know that I'm not going to call him with you standing right there," I said.

"I know, I know," he replied, as he reluctantly walked back around the house and through the side door.

I was alone now. The time had finally come. I looked down at Ronnie's phone and pulled up Brandon's number. For twenty-seven long years, I had wanted to talk to my son, as any mother wants to talk to her children, and now I was only the push of a button from doing just that. What a miracle this was! This was literally going to be a life-changing phone call. It would be a long-distance call, all right, but it would span a lot more than merely six hundred miles. This phone call would reach across two worlds and almost three decades.

I took a deep breath and hit the call button. It rang a couple of times before a young man answered the phone, "Hello."

Now I could tell you about his deep voice, or his vague southern accent, but the truth is, the only thing I really heard was him crying all over again as if we were back in 1984. Just from hearing his voice, my mind instantly raced back to that hospital delivery room where he had been taken from me so many years ago. I was speechless. He may have grown into young man, but he was still my child.

I was awakened from my daydream by, "Hello, can you hear me?" Recovering quickly, I said, "Brandon?"

"Hey, it's me," he said. I could tell by the tone of his voice that he was just as nervous as I was. There certainly wasn't a handbook for any of this. "So, how are you doing with all of this?" he asked.

"I'm extremely happy," I replied. "Nervous but happy."

The two of us trying to make conversation seemed to be the epitome of an oxymoron. We were mother and son, and yet we were total strangers. It was obvious after the first few minutes that someone was going to have to break the ice. Finally, Brandon spoke up and said, "Look, I'm just going to be honest. I'm nervous, and I know that you are too, but I think that the only way to move forward is to be transparent and honest, so I'll go first. I want you to know that I have no hard feelings at all toward you, and no matter what you tell me about the past, I won't hold it against you. I just want to know what happened."

I was relieved and grateful for the invitation to explain myself without the fear of judgment, because I didn't see how I could justifiably explain to my child why I had given him up. I began to tell him the whole story of my irresponsible choices and how I had gotten pregnant when I was nineteen. I explained how Mom had set up the closed adoption. I also walked him through that horrible day at the hospital when we were separated, and how I had always hoped that this day would come.

It was clear that he was hungry for answers about his past and understandably so. No sooner had I answered his first question than he came in with another one: "What about my birth father?"

I explained to him that we had dated for a short time and that we had broken up not long before I'd found out I was pregnant—and that I had never told him about the pregnancy. I assured Brandon that I would do whatever I could to find his father if he wanted me to, but he said, "Maybe sometime down the road I will look for him, but I just want to focus on us right now." That was just fine by me.

When I got through explaining the details surrounding the pregnancy, he asked me, "Did you ever try to find me?" Believe it or not, I had made it up to this point without crying, but when he asked me that question, the dam broke. In tears, I replied, "There hasn't been a day go by that I haven't thought about you, but I never tried to find you, because I felt as if I had signed away my rights as a mother. I thought that I had no business barging into your life or the lives of your family."

He took a moment as if to gather himself, and then he replied, "It's okay. You have absolutely nothing to feel bad about. I was just trying to make conversation." I had worried so much through the years that he hated me, but he was starting to convince me that he really didn't have any hard feelings. I was now beginning to get my sea legs up under me concerning this conversation. It was time for me to ask some questions now.

"So, Brandon, let me ask *you* a question. Why did you want to find me? Were you just curious about the past, or do you really want to establish some type of a relationship?"

He replied, "Well, if it's okay with you, I would like for us to have a healthy mother-son relationship. I think it would be nice if one day I could feel like the son who moved off and got married."

"That's exactly what I want," I said, trying to hide that fact that my heart was melting inside of me. I took this opening in the conversation to jump in and share my heart with him. I said, "Brandon, I really mean what I'm about to say. I want you to know that even having never met you, I have always loved you. There has never been a doubt in my mind about that. I love you just as much as my other children. I love all my children equally and that includes you. I promise you that, no matter how long it takes, I'm going to prove that to you."

I was taken aback by his response. "I'm not going to lie," he said. "I do have some insecurities that I'm going to have to work through, but I really do believe you. It took me a long time to come to this conclusion, but I want you to know that I believe that your giving me up for adoption *was* an act of love. You sacrificed and did your best for me, just like you did for your other children, even though it was different." I knew when he made that statement that we were both on the same page and reaching for the same goal. All those years of guilt and worry over the effect the adoption would have on him faded away with those words.

I then asked him how in the world he had found me after all these years. He told me the whole story about running into problems with the sealed records and about how he was able to see through the permanent marker to get just enough information to find me. I thought it was amazing. It certainly seemed like much more than a coincidence. I had no idea how true that would prove to be.

The conversation then shifted to our immediate concerns. We were both worried about how our relationship would affect those in our immediate families. He was worried about my other children, and I was worried about his parents. We both reassured one another that everyone was happy about us finding each other and that we were secure in our relationships. With that cleared, it seemed that all of the roadblocks and speed bumps in the road to our relationship were removed. Now all we had to do was move forward.

With all of those nagging questions out of the way, we really began to open up and talk about ourselves and our lives. For about the next three hours, we both laughed and cried together, as we attempted to catch up on twenty-seven years. There were definitely some losses that had to be acknowledged, a lot of memories that we would never get to share with one another. However, we both conceded the bittersweet fact that we had led good lives apart from one another. We were just thankful for this second chance, and we knew that we needed to look ahead.

As it got late and the conversation began to wind down, we talked about the possibility of a reunion, although we didn't set a place or a date. We were just about to get off the phone for the night when he said something that I will never forget. "Can I ask you one last question?"

"Sure," I replied.

"Please don't think me crazy for saying this, but the truth is that I would feel extremely weird and disrespectful for calling you by your first name, so would it be all right if I call you Mom?"

My heart jumped for joy inside of my chest! "I would love that," I replied. "I just want to make sure that your mom won't get offended."

"No, I don't think she will mind at all. She knows that it's no disrespect to her," he said.

What a wonderful way to cap off one the greatest moments of my life. This was just too good to be true!

We told one another that we loved each other and said our good-byes before we hung up the phone. I sat there by myself on the porch for a few minutes, trying to process what had just happened. I was expecting any minute to wake out of my sleep, thus exiting this wonderful dream. But it was really happening!

I eventually got up and walked inside. After entering through the front door, I headed to the bedroom, where Ronnie was already in bed. He wasn't asleep, though. As soon as I walked in, he said, "Well?"

I recited the conversation for him the best I could, while I changed and got into bed. It all just seemed like a blur. I guess good stress can wear you out just as much as bad stress. I was exhausted, and after giving Ronnie the "Cliffs Notes" version of our conversation, I drifted off into a deep sleep.

Brandon's Perspective

In the moments after we got off the phone, I sat there in the bedroom recliner, just staring at the floor. For the first time in my life, I had just talked to the woman who had brought me into this world. Just to hear the love in her voice did something to me that I can't even begin to explain. When she'd given me up for adoption, she hadn't been in a position to take care of me. She hadn't *wanted* to give me up. And now we had been given a second chance. I felt so blessed. I sat there, wondering how many people live their entire lives and never have an opportunity like the one that had been placed before us: a chance to right the wrongs and mend the fences, a chance to go back in time and deal fate a devastating blow. I couldn't help but feel that I was a part of something so much bigger than myself. Things like this don't just happen; they are divinely orchestrated.

Eventually, I got up and headed down the hallway and into

our living room, where Leah was on the couch watching TV. She immediately turned the TV off when I entered the room and said, "Tell me all about it."

I repeated all of the conversation that I could think of. Needless to say, with so many years to catch up on, we talked about a lot without really even scratching the surface. I had briefly shared some of my testimony with my birth mom, but I hadn't gone into too much detail. I couldn't wait until we got a little closer so I could share what the Lord had done for me—how He had saved me and called me into the ministry. Even early on, it was heavy on my heart to share the gospel with her. But the Lord also set it in my heart to let her lead and ask the questions. So that's what I did.

After Leah and I talked for a little while, we headed off to bed. We were going to get up and go to church the next morning, so we didn't want to be up too late. It didn't take me long before I was out for the count.

The next day was a special time for me. I got to stand up in front of our church and share the wonderful news with everyone. We have an extremely tight-knit church family, and it was wonderful to be able to rejoice with them. It was apparent to everyone that the Lord was up to something, and indeed He was.

After the morning service we grabbed a bite to eat and headed to Mom's house to hang out before the night service. We live almost an hour from our church, so it's the usual custom to go to Mom's house, since she lives a lot closer. As soon as we got settled in, I got on the computer to check my Facebook account. When I signed on, I noticed that I had three new "friend requests." To my surprise, they were requests from Devin, Forrest, and Amber, but they didn't just ask me to be their friend. They asked me to be their brother. That meant that, from then on, whenever someone looked at their Facebook page, I would show up as their brother. That may not mean a whole lot to you, but it brought me to tears. I guess that was their simple way of saying, "Welcome to the family."

Like most good Baptists, my family and I like to take a nap on Sunday afternoons, and this Sunday was no exception. After a while, everyone was zonked out. I took this opportunity to call my birth mom and continue on with our conversation.

I didn't think my day could get any better, but not long after my birth mom and I began talking, she said, "Hold on a minute." A few seconds later, she came back to the phone and said, "Hey, Devin said he wants to talk to you for a minute if that's okay."

"Sure, put him on," I said, beginning to get a little nervous.

A few seconds later, Devin answered, "Hey, Brandon, how's everything going, man?"

"I don't think I could be any better," I said.

"That's great," he replied. I then chimed in with the one question that was burning in my heart. "Devin, I want you to be honest with me. How do you feel about this whole thing with me coming into the picture? I know it must have been a huge deal to you and the siblings." I'll never forget what Devin said next.

"This is a miracle, Brandon. We're all happy about it, not just Mom. Don't feel at all like you're intruding. You're my brother. You're family." It took every bit of manly pride in me not to get emotional, but I managed not to.

We chit-chatted for a while longer, and then he handed the phone back to my birth mom. She and I talked for about another hour or so before we said our good-byes. We agreed to talk at least a little bit every day, if possible. We knew, however, that while we had our heads in the clouds, we still had to keep our feet on the ground. We both had families and jobs, not to mention the fact that we had a ten-hour drive separating the two of us. Reality doesn't stop, even for a dream come true.

That was, no doubt, one of the greatest weekends of my life. What a miracle this was, and it was just getting started! I just couldn't help but wonder what the next step would be.

Cheryl's Perspective

After I got off the phone with Brandon, I went into the kitchen and began to cook. We had friends coming over in a little while to watch the Super Bowl, and I had a lot that had to be done. I was dying inside as I grated cheese to make the nacho dip. Although it was one of the greatest experiences of my life talking to my son, I was still miserable. It wasn't that I was ungrateful. I wasn't. You just have to understand that I had never *seen* my son! The closest I had ever come to laying eyes on him was that Polaroid that the nurse had given me back in 1984. But it had long since been misplaced over the years. I had never held him or kissed him—or been able to do any of those motherly things for that matter. And now I knew where he was. The only reason I hadn't already jumped into a car or on a plane was because I didn't want to seem too forward. After all, he did have a life and a family of his own. But honestly, how much can a mother take?

It wasn't long before all of our guests began to arrive. Our living room was now full of people talking and laughing and just having a good time. I, on the other hand, was sitting on the couch in my own little depressed world. The Patriots and Giants were playing, and it was a good game, but I couldn't have cared less. I dwelled on my misery until I didn't think I could take it anymore.

Suddenly, Ronnie got up from his recliner and headed to the kitchen. As he walked in front of me, I grabbed his pant leg and motioned for him to come in close. As he bent down, I quietly asked him, "Ronnie, would you do me a big favor?"

"Sure," he said.

"Will you take me to Alabama this weekend?"

He replied, "Let's do it."

15
Two Worlds Collide: Part 1

Friday, February 10, 2012
Brandon's Perspective

Five days had now come and gone since my birth mom had point-blank asked me if it would be okay if she and Ronnie drove up to meet us over the weekend. The Sunday night when she asked me that question was the first time it really sank in how much she actually *did* care about me. We had just spoken for the first time the day before, and now she wanted to make the ten-hour drive just to see me. I definitely wanted to meet her, but I didn't want to overstep my bounds. Besides that, with my work and church schedule, it wasn't like I could randomly take off anytime I wanted to. Needless to say, I was so excited that she was coming to Alabama!

Their plans were to get off work early on Thursday and drive to Tallahassee, which is about the halfway point. They would stay the night there and head out the next morning. Friday was now here, and Leah and I were expecting them to pull in at about 4:30 p.m. I had made it through a long work week and an even longer workday, but in just a matter of hours, I was going to be face-to-face for the first time with the woman who had brought me into the world. All of the preparations had been made, and now it was just a waiting game. I don't think I've ever been so nervous in my life. What would I say? What would I do?

Cheryl's Perspective

I've never thought of a GPS device as being a type of hourglass, but that was exactly what it seemed like to me as we headed up the interstate. We typed in Brandon's Gordo address just before we pulled out of the hotel parking lot, and with every passing mile, the remaining trip time got smaller and smaller. The GPS had us pulling into their driveway at about 4:00 p.m., which translated to about 4:30 p.m. with pit stops.

We crossed the Alabama state line about 1:00 p.m. The palm trees and Spanish moss were now beginning to give way to large pines and hardwoods, and my anxiety kicked up another notch with this indicator of how close we were getting. You would think that a mother going to see her son would be the most natural thing in the world, but I was so on-edge. This wasn't quite a normal visit.

As the hours went by, the sand remaining in the hourglass got smaller and smaller. We were just about thirty minutes from Gordo, when we came into the Tuscaloosa city limits. I perked up and began to look around. It was a fairly large college town with a population of around three hundred thousand. It didn't really seem that different from any other city I had seen, but it intrigued me to see with my own eyes the place where my son had grown up. For all these years, I had wondered about where he was, and now my mind had a picture of that very place. It was here that we stopped one last time to use the restroom and freshen up before making the short drive to Gordo.

We got back onto the highway and eventually made our way out of the city limits. Woods and swampland were now the only things in sight as we headed west down Highway 82. It was now the dead of winter, and the trees were completely barren of any leaves. It was rather cold outside—much different from what we were used to in central Florida. It was in the thirties and was predicted to dip into the lower teens overnight.

Twenty minutes, ten minutes, five minutes—the arrival time

was getting closer and closer. We passed a sign that said, "Gordo, 2 Miles," and I could feel my palms beginning to sweat. Two miles later, we entered the town of Gordo, and I really felt as if I was going to be sick. Ronnie even asked me if he needed to pull over, but I declined as I tried to pull myself together. We made our way through the small town of Gordo as we neared our destination. With its one traffic light, well-kept neighborhoods, and a handful of small stores, Gordo reminded me of the town of Mayberry from the *Andy Griffith Show*.

We took a right on 2nd Street NW. The GPS now said that we were just seven tenths of a mile from our destination. I tried my best to be calm and tell myself that there was nothing to be nervous about, but it was just easier said than done. I could feel my heart about to beat out of my chest as we got ever so close.

Brandon's Perspective

The clock on the microwave read 4:36 p.m. I was camped out in the kitchen, staring out the window at the driveway. Ronnie had called me about thirty minutes ago when they were going through Tuscaloosa. They *had* to be getting close. For about the past ten minutes, I would glance out the window, pace around the kitchen for a minute, and repeat. Now my eyes were locked on the driveway, knowing that I would see their car at any second. I don't get worked up about much, but I was absolutely sick to my stomach.

I stood there, trying to come up with a general idea of what I wanted to say and do when we first met, but I was shaken from my thoughts when I saw their black Ford Fusion pull into the driveway. "They're here!" I shouted to Leah, who was in the back of the house. "Would you please get the door?" I asked her in a shaky voice. I still don't really understand why, but I didn't want to be the one to answer the door. I wanted my birth mom to be in the house before I walked in to see her. Perhaps I wanted to make sure that we were in the privacy of our home before we engaged in this emotional reunion, but I'm not sure. It's funny how your mind works in intense situations like that.

Cheryl's Perspective

Ronnie and I got out of the car and began to head to the carport door. The cold wind was cutting at us like a knife, but I was too high on adrenaline to care. I walked up the few steps leading up to the door and knocked. A few seconds later, Leah appeared. With a big smile, she said, "It's so good to see you. Come on in and get out of the cold." As soon as I stepped into the living room, I saw Wesley and Ally. They were beautiful, and they were staring at us as if to say, "Who are you?" I quickly scanned the room but didn't see Brandon anywhere.

No sooner had Ronnie shut the door behind him than Brandon appeared out of the kitchen. There he was, the one whose cries had haunted me for almost thirty years. There he was, the one I had seen so many times in my mind—and now *finally* with my eyes. There he was! I couldn't believe that it was really him!

We both stood there for a moment, just staring at one another. It was as if both of us had something to say but couldn't say it. We had things that we wanted to do, but we couldn't do them. The battle raging inside of *me* was between the hysterical mother and the respectful stranger. I wanted to squeeze him so tightly that he couldn't breathe, but I didn't want to scare him. However, within just a few seconds, the hysterical mom took over. I walked over and wrapped my arms around him, burying my face in his shoulder.

We stood there embracing one another for what seemed like an eternity, while Ronnie and Leah looked on, teary-eyed. It was almost completely silent. The only sound was my muffled crying. It was one of those rare moments in life where there seems to be so much to say, and yet the silence says it all. I knew that I couldn't stand there and hold him forever, but it was as if I was somehow making up for letting him go all those years ago. I believed in my heart that giving him up for adoption had been the best thing for him, but I selfishly knew that if I had to do it all over again, there was no way I would let him go. I would have done whatever it took to keep him. However, none of that was relevant at the moment. I had him now, and that was all that mattered.

Brandon's Perspective

I couldn't believe that I was standing there in my living room holding my birth mom. I was just overwhelmed with joy! There was completeness in that moment that was different from anything I'd ever known. I wish there were stronger words in the dictionary to describe the way I felt, but that's just the best I can do. To see us together in that moment, one would never have thought that there was ever a time that she couldn't or wouldn't have kept me. Growing up, I had often wondered if she ever thought about me or if she loved me. Within about five seconds of meeting her, every ounce of doubt had been removed.

Eventually we let go, and when we did, her knees buckled. I had to grab her to keep her from falling. I guess the emotion of the situation was just overwhelming. She was fine, though—just a little woozy. We all made our way over to the couch and began to tone things down a bit. We started with small talk about how their trip had gone and how unusually cold the weather was—just general stuff.

My birth mom took this time to give Wesley and Allie some gifts that she and Ronnie had bought for them. And like normal toddlers, they took the toys out and began to play inside the ever-entertaining bag. It was cute, and we all burst into laughter. I then looked at Wesley and Allie and said, "Tell them thank you." It then occurred to me that they would need to know whom they were thanking. I asked Ronnie and my birth mom, "So, what do you want them to call you?"

"Paw Paw and Mimi will work just fine," they replied. "Thank you, Paw Paw and Mimi," said the kids in innocent voices. I really thought it was great that the kids would grow up knowing my birth family—and vice versa.

After we all got settled in, I walked to the closet and got out the old photo albums that I had borrowed from Mom, because I knew that my birth mom would probably want to be filled in on my life up to this point.

Cheryl's Perspective

Brandon sat down next to me and opened up a large photo album. We started from the very beginning. He first showed me the pictures of the adoption ceremony from when he was just two months old. I had regained control of my emotions after sitting down and conversing for a while, but as soon as I saw those pictures, I began to tear up again. The faces of his parents were glowing with joy as they held him for the first time. Brandon looked just like Devin in his baby pictures. The only difference was that *I* was with Devin in *his* baby pictures. Don't get me wrong: I have nothing but the utmost respect for Brandon's parents. I'm so grateful to them for doing for him what I couldn't do. The only battle going on was between me, myself, and I.

For the next two hours, we took a stroll down memory lane. We looked at yearbooks, photos, and home videos. It was kind of strange that, although Brandon had looked like Devin in his younger days, he began to look a lot like Forrest as he grew older. There's only one way to describe how it felt to sit there with Brandon and catch up on his life: painfully awesome. It was painfully awesome to see my son in all the Kodak moments of his life, yet having missed every one of them. I felt like the scum of the earth. There was an unavoidable battle between joy and regret going on inside of me. But I'd known it was coming and that it was something I'd just have to work through.

All of a sudden, Ronnie broke the mood with a loud clap of his hands. "So, where are we gonna eat? I'm starving." It was a nice transition from the intense seriousness. Ronnie has a habit of doing that. We eventually decided to eat at Logan's in Tuscaloosa. Brandon and his family loaded up in their car, and Ronnie and I followed them in our car. We all would have ridden together, but I had made up my mind that I wasn't going to take any chances on making them feel uncomfortable by staying the night with them. Ronnie and I had decided that we would stay at a hotel in Tuscaloosa.

For the rest of the night, everything seemed rather normal. It was the closest thing to a normal family dinner that you could expect, given the circumstances. I must admit, however, that I couldn't quit staring at Brandon. Just as I had stared at his picture in the office that day, I kept looking at him, thinking to myself, *I can't believe it's really him!* Brandon never did say anything about it, but he *had* to have noticed.

After we ate at Logan's, we checked into the hotel just a block away. We all went to our room and chatted for a while before calling it a night. We were all exhausted, so we agreed to get a good night's rest and start again the next day. We had the whole day planned out and couldn't wait to get started.

Brandon's Perspective

Just before we said good-bye, my birth mom looked at me and said, "Brandon, do you think there will be a time tomorrow that I can meet your mom?"

I was somewhat surprised by the request, but I don't suppose I should have been. "Sure," I said. "I bet she would like that. I'll call her and see if there is a time tomorrow that will be good for her."

"Good," she replied, and with that we said our good-nights and headed back to Gordo.

The next morning, we drove to the hotel to pick up Ronnie and my birth mom. I must say that I think all of us felt and looked better than we had the day before. The stress and anticipation of the reunion had taken its toll on everyone. When we got to the hotel, I got out and left the car running so that Leah and the kids would stay warm. It was absolutely freezing outside—unusually cold even for winter in Alabama. I knocked on the door, and they were already waiting for me. We all hurried to the car to get out of the cold. I felt so sorry for them, because they hadn't packed any warm clothes at all. It was easy to tell that they were from central Florida.

From start to finish, that was one of the best days of my life. For the next few hours, I drove them around and gave them a tour of my life. We went by the two houses that I grew up in, my school, and the church where I had gotten saved and married. It was a special time.

After we ate lunch, we headed to Mom's house. I had called her that morning, and she'd said that she would love to meet my birth mom and Ronnie if we could come around 1:00 p.m. I must admit that I was a little nervous about the meeting. It was nothing against either one of my moms. It's just that there is no manual for any of these things, so I just wasn't sure how it would go.

We got out of the car and knocked on the door. Mom opened the door, and we all briskly walked inside and shut the door before anyone introduced themselves. Ronnie and Mom introduced themselves first. But when my birth mom went to introduce *herself*, something took place that I didn't really expect to see. She went up to Mom and gave her a big hug and tearfully said, "Thank you. Thank you so much for doing what I couldn't do and for taking good care of my son." My mom, who isn't a very emotional person at all, began crying, and she replied, "No, thank *you* for doing the hard thing and giving him up for adoption. It's been a joy to raise him all of these years."

That image of my two moms hugging and thanking one another will always be burned into my mind. Just when I didn't think it could possibly get any better, my birth mom pulled some flowers and a card out of a bag she'd brought in and handed it to Mom. My mom thanked her, and then she said, "Wait here one second, because I have something that I want to give *you.*" With that, she went back to her bedroom to retrieve the gift.

I was at full attention now. My mom hadn't even known that we were coming over until that morning, so I had no idea that she had gotten her a gift. A few minutes later, Mom walked out and handed my birth mom my first outfit: the one they had taken me home in. They hugged again, both crying heavily now. It was all I could do to keep any semblance of manliness. I'd had no idea that Mom even had my baby outfit, much less that she had planned on giving it to my birth mom. What a special moment!

We sat around and talked a little while. The moms seemed to have a lot to catch up on as well. Mothers have a special language when it comes to their children. My birth mom was trying to find out all she could about me from the one who had raised me—a dangerous situation, I know. I felt so privileged to have two moms who loved me. I just sat back and listened as they talked. I can't help but laugh a little when I think about what would ever happen to me if I made them both mad. Imagine having *two* moms mad at you!

After a while, we told Mom good-bye and headed on our way. We wanted to get rested up before dinner. Mom was going to meet up back up with us that evening and was take us all out to the Cypress Inn, a nice seafood restaurant on the Black Warrior River. It was just a special day from beginning to end.

Later that night when day was finally over, we drove Ronnie and my birth mom back to the hotel. They were getting up early in the morning and driving back home, so we all agreed to say our good-byes that night. I hugged Ronnie and my birth mom good-bye. She did her absolute best not to get emotional, but you could tell that she didn't want to leave. To comfort her, I gave her a promise that we would drive down to Florida the next month and meet everyone. It seemed to comfort her a little. We said our emotional good-byes and headed home. It made me sick to see her go after such a short time, but I felt guilty for letting myself be ungrateful. I just had to look forward to the next visit.

As awesome as the weekend had been, Leah and I both knew that the Lord was just getting started. We knew that He was up to something, and I couldn't wait to see what it was. Our trip to Florida couldn't get there fast enough!

16
Two Worlds Collide: Part 2

March 29, 2012
Brandon's Perspective

IT WAS A THURSDAY MORNING, AND we were well on our way to Winter Haven, Florida. We had driven to Tallahassee the day before, stayed the night, and left in the morning. Our plans were to arrive in the early afternoon on Thursday and head back home on Sunday morning. I couldn't believe that six weeks had already flown by since my birth mom and Ronnie had come to visit. I was elated about meeting the rest of my family! This was an absolute dream come true.

We were only about two hours away from Winter Haven when the first amazing event of our trip took place. Now I don't believe in asking God for a sign, but in this case He gave us one anyway. It was a sign, literally. We were somewhere near Gainesville, the place where I had been born, when we saw a billboard that sent a chill up my spine. This pro-life billboard had a picture of a pregnant woman standing sideways, while the hand of God was coming out of the sky and touching her belly. The sign simply read, "Before I formed thee in the belly, I knew thee" (Jeremiah 1:5).

When I saw that, my mind instantly raced back to that day in my senior high Bible class where I had run across this life-changing verse. Leah and I looked at one another and smiled. I said, "You just can't make this stuff up." She knew exactly what I was talking about, for I had rehearsed the story to her before. We must have seen that same billboard five times before we reached our destination. You can call it a coincidence if you want to, but I know better. I'd known from the beginning that the Lord had His hand in my finding my family, and I needed no confirmation, but it was as if God was reiterating the fact that He was up to something.

As we neared their house, I began to get somewhat nervous about meeting all of the siblings and the rest of the family, but the anxiety wasn't even in the same ball park as when I first met my birth mom. There was just a more relaxed feeling about this trip—not to mention the fact that the weather was gorgeous. There was nothing but blue skies and sunshine with mild temperatures. I couldn't wait to get there!

Cheryl's Perspective

We had spent the past few days preparing sleeping accommodations, cleaning house, and stocking up on food. Now the time was almost here. It just seemed like an absolute dream come true, the kind of thing that you only see in the movies. Even though all four of my children had never even met, I just knew in my heart that they would have a good relationship from the start. I just couldn't believe that all four of my children would be together and happy. For the first time ever, all of my children would be sleeping under my roof, eating at my table, and conversing in my living room—not to mention the fact that Leah and the grandbabies were coming! It was almost more than a mother could take!

We had the whole weekend planned out. When they arrived, they would get to meet Devin for the first time. We planned on getting acquainted that afternoon and allowing Brandon and his family to rest after the long trip. That night we would all drive to the Olive Garden in Orlando, where Forrest and Amber would meet us for dinner. We had pretty much left Friday free to do whatever we wanted to, and then that night we were all having a family dinner at the house. All of the relatives were coming over. It was going to be like a Thanksgiving dinner without the turkey. Then, on Saturday, I wanted to take Brandon on a tour of my life as he had done for me in Alabama. They had planned to leave early on Sunday morning, because we all had to be back at work on Monday.

There were no nerves left over from the trip to Alabama. It really *did* feel like the son who had married and moved away was coming home for a visit—only this would be much more special. I was expecting them to pull up any minute. I would stop my last-minute preparations every few minutes to walk over to the living room window and take a peek.

Brandon's Perspective

We made our way into Winter Haven a little after 2:00 p.m. It looked like a nice little community, full of vacation homes and lakefront property. However, it was difficult to tell where one community ended and another one began. All of the towns seem to run together. In West Alabama, most of the towns were separated by miles of woods. After weaving our way through town, we turned into their neighborhood. It was an older neighborhood that had been well-maintained. The lawns were very well-kept and landscaped, and there were palm trees everywhere. I was getting excited as I made my final turn onto Meadowlark Court.

As we pulled into the driveway, Mom ran out to meet us. She seemed almost giddy with excitement, as were we. After we hugged, I looked up to see Devin walk out the front door of the house along with Ronnie.

Devin met me halfway up the sidewalk and gave me a big hug. I thought that it might be an extremely emotional moment, but, although it was a special event in my life, it just seemed rather—normal. That's the only way I know how to describe it. It was just like I was seeing my little brother after being away for a while. There was nothing weird about it. We shared small talk about our trip for a minute as he helped us to unload the car.

As I made my way into the house, I was struck with a feeling of déjà vu, almost as if I had seen this place before in a dream or something. The whole experience of "coming home" was so strangely normal. I couldn't wait to see what the rest of the week held for all of us.

That night it was much the same. A few minutes after we were seated at the Olive Garden, Forrest and Amber arrived, and it was just as normal meeting them as it had been meeting Devin. It was like a normal family meal. We talked and caught up on things, just as if I had been away on a trip. It's hard to describe how powerful that normalcy was. It was a testament to the degree to which my siblings had accepted me as their brother.

That week was, no doubt, one of the best of my life—not because we did anything extraordinary but because we had a chance to enjoy all of the common things together. The next morning, we got up and eased into the day, much to my liking. We just relaxed while watching TV and talking. After that, we headed out to lunch at their favorite pizzeria. We then took the kids to a really nice park just down from where we'd eaten lunch. It was awesome to see Ronnie, Mom, and my siblings play with Wesley and Allie. They seemed thrilled to be able to spend time with their grandkids/niece and nephew. That old saying, "It's not what you're doing; it's who you're with," began to take on a whole new meaning as we did all those normal, everyday things together. I couldn't help but feel so blessed for having been given this opportunity.

That night after we had all gotten settled in, the company began to arrive. The house was now full of relatives that I had never met: aunts, uncles, cousins, and even my grandmother. They were all very kind to me, and it was a pleasure to meet them.

After everyone had eaten, we played a few games of *Phase 10* and *Skip-Bo*. We were just about to begin a new game, when Ronnie's sister Sherry spoke up and said, "Brandon, don't you play the guitar?"

"Yes, ma'am, I try," I replied with a chuckle.

"Well why don't you and Forrest play a song for us?"

Forrest said, "That's good with me, if you want to, Brandon."

"We'll give it a try anyway," I replied.

Forrest disappeared down the hall for a few seconds and reappeared with his violin in hand. As I was pulling my guitar out of the case, he asked me, "So, what song would you like to play?"

"Do you know 'Amazing Grace' in C?" I asked.

"Sure thing," he replied. "Let's try it."

We got tuned up as the room began to quiet down. All eyes were now on us as we began to play. Hearing "Amazing Grace" on the violin was one of the most beautiful sounds that had ever hit my ears, and the way Forrest played it certainly did it justice. He is a gifted musician. It was a powerful moment as we played that song together. There was definitely a "holy hush" factor involved. Picture that scene: the family watching two brothers, who had just been miraculously reunited, playing a tribute to the reason behind it. The only reason that we were all gathered there that day was because of the amazing grace of almighty God! That was one of the most precious moments of my life.

After we got done playing, Mom spoke up and said, "Don't move, you two. Stay right there." She then began digging through some drawers in the living room until she pulled out an old hymnal. She sat down beside us, and for the next hour, we played and sang some of her old favorites that she had learned as a child in church. Mom had a pretty singing voice, and it was fun to have a sing-along.

Eventually all of the company left, and the immediate family stayed up late playing card games, as well as the Wii. We were like a bunch of energetic teenagers as we played into the early morning hours before finally making our way to bed—which was unusual for me on *any* day of the week. From beginning to end, it was just a great day.

The next day, Mom took us on a tour of her life. She showed us some of her memorable places. She took us to see her high school and the house she'd grown up in—the place where she'd lived when she was pregnant with me. It was intriguing to me to see all of these places that I had tried to picture in my mind so many times before.

We all kind of took it easy on that Saturday afternoon. I was glad, because everyone was worn-out, and we were going to get up early the next day and make the ten-hour drive back to Gordo.

That night before we all went to bed was probably the highlight of the trip. We were all sitting in the living room, talking, just kind of rehashing the week. Although the week had gone incredibly well, I was still dying to get something off my chest. I wanted to hear straight from my siblings that they were okay with me coming into their lives and that they weren't just putting on to make Mom happy. Looking back, I realize that I was just putting too much pressure on myself, but I'm glad that I broke all of the ice.

After a while of small talk, I finally spoke up. "Well, Forrest, Amber, and Devin, I have a question that I want to ask you."

"Sure," they replied, now giving me their undivided attention.

"After I found out that Mom wanted me in her life but she hadn't even told you guys about me, I have been worried sick about kind of wedging myself into your lives." I really didn't have any idea that I would get emotional, but it began to pour out of me like a fire hydrant. However, I continued on. "It just seems like y'all have such a good family, and I don't want to mess that up," I said tearfully.

They each began to speak up, one at a time, to give their input. Devin went first. "Brandon, you're my brother, and Leah is my sister-in-law, and Wesley and Allie are my niece and nephew. You guys are family, and I'm glad that this weekend is just the start!" I could tell from his emotion that he meant every word he said.

Amber then spoke up. She didn't get two words into her first sentence before she started to get very emotional. "When Mom told me that I had a brother I didn't know about, it really hurt me. I kept wondering why you weren't with us. I just felt that you should have been with us growing up, and after this week, I feel even stronger about that. I feel like, in just a few days' time, I have gotten close to you and Leah, as well as the kids. So you shouldn't feel that way at all."

Tears were flowing all around the room now. Ronnie got up to "go to the bathroom," but we all knew the he didn't want us to see him cry.

The mood only subsided when Forrest, with a confused look on his face, spoke up and said, "Wait a minute. You're telling me that we have to see you again? I thought this was just a onetime deal." His timely sarcasm left us all in a roar of laughter. Forrest isn't an emotional person at all, but his sarcasm spoke volumes. I knew what he meant.

Cheryl's Perspective

As a mother, I was in an absolute state of euphoria all week long. It was such a great week, getting to spend quality time with all of my children, but nothing could have topped this. I sat there quietly in the recliner as I watched my children have this deeply personal dialogue. Up to this point, their relationship had existed only through a mediator: me. Now they were opening up and making themselves vulnerable in order to draw closer to one another. I didn't say a word until I knew that they were finished, because I didn't want to get in their way.

When I realized that they were completely done, it was time for me to make *my* move. "Well I was going to do this tomorrow before you guys left, but I believe now would be the perfect time. Brandon, do you remember saying to me that you wanted to feel like the son who had married and moved away?"

"Yes, ma'am," he replied.

"I've got something that I want to give you to help in that process," I said. I then pulled out a house key I'd had made just for him and placed it in his hand. "You may not get to use it much because we are so far away. But maybe it will serve as a reminder that you always have a home and a family down here." He began sobbing almost uncontrollably. I'd had no idea that a simple house key could mean so much. What a perfect exclamation mark to put on such a wonderful week!

Brandon's Perspective

We finally made our way to bed after we had said our good-nights. As I lay on my pillow, I felt so relieved that not only did my birth mom love me and want me in the family, but so did my siblings. The key Mom had given me was a tangible relic that I could hold in my hand to be reminded of this truth.

The next morning, we got up around seven and began to load the car. The mood was so much different from the way it had been all week. We knew that a good-bye was looming near. Everyone was kind of quiet as they helped us load our luggage.

We all gathered outside, where it was surprisingly cool. We all embraced and said our good-byes, trying to keep it upbeat and happy. It was hard for all of us, especially Mom. Once again, we made plans to see each other. This time, the whole family planned on coming up to Alabama in April. That gave us something to look forward to. We all kept it together pretty well until I began to back out of the driveway, and then Mom lost it. Amber, seeing this, gave her a big hug. We waved good-bye as we headed back to Alabama.

Cheryl's Perspective

I was so mad at myself as they disappeared around the corner—mad that I had lost control of my emotions, and full of regret about this pain I was feeling. I knew it would get easier, but that didn't help me at the moment. I was always going to second-guess myself about the adoption to some degree, that was for sure.

I walked inside and went straight to our bedroom, shutting the door behind me. I had to get a grip. It had been a wonderful week, and I would see Brandon and his family again soon. I kept telling that to myself until I actually felt better. We had the rest of our lives to catch up. I just had to be patient. I would be on my way to Alabama again before I knew it!

17
Reconciled

But when the fullness of the time was come, God sent
forth his Son, made of a woman, made under the law,
to redeem them that were under the law, that we might
receive the adoption of sons.
—Galatians 4:4–5

May 26, 2012
Brandon's Perspective

OVER THE PAST FEW MONTHS, MY birth mom and I had really
made a lot of headway in our relationship. Between talking
almost every day, their trip to Alabama, and our trip to Florida, we
had grown a lot closer. The whole family also made a trip to our
house in April for a few days. That was an awesome experience.
They even came to our church to hear me preach while they were
here.

As we got closer and opened up about pretty much all aspects of
our lives, one thing became clear to me: the Lord was dealing with
my mom's heart about salvation. It was no surprise to me, because
we had a lot of people on my end who were praying for her. Mom
had been raised in the Church of Christ as a young girl, and just
like me, she had been baptized into their church. But she didn't

have a testimony of salvation, and she hadn't been to church in any capacity for almost twenty years.

We hadn't been talking but just a couple of weeks when she asked about my faith for the first time. She told me that she had tried to take the kids to the Church of Christ when they were little, but she just didn't see much of a point. When I didn't say much, she just point-blank asked me, "So what made you change from the Church of Christ to being a Baptist?"

I took this opportunity to give her my testimony about how the Lord had saved me. I then shared the gospel with her and told her how to be saved. She listened intently, not saying much at all. When I was finished talking, she said, "Well I'm definitely going to chew on that for a while, but I know one thing for sure: your whole voice changed when you talked about your faith. There is a tone of excitement in your voice, and I know that it's real to you."

As time went on, her questions became more frequent and more thought-out. I recall another conversation where she had actually written down questions throughout the day so that she would remember to ask me the next time that we talked. The question on her list that stuck out to me the most was, "So where does a person's soul go when he dies?" I explained to her that the saved person who has repented and put his faith in Christ's perfect sacrifice for his sin goes to heaven to be with the Lord; but the lost person who rejects Christ must go to hell to pay for his own sin.

It was obvious that she was pondering the things of eternity, but she hadn't quite gotten it yet. She would often say things like, "Well I know that I need to get back in church," to which I replied, "Mom, just going to church never got anybody to heaven."

One time she said, "I know that I need to be a better person." I told her, "Being a good person never made anybody right with God. Hell is full of good people." My comments threw her off a little bit, but that was exactly what I wanted to do. I didn't want her to put faith in the wrong things. She never brushed me off; she always took what I said and pondered it.

The day that the gospel shined its glorious light in her heart for the first time was on May 26, 2012. It was a Saturday that I will never forget as long as I live. It was Memorial Day weekend, and Mom had flown up by herself on that Friday to spend some time with us. That Saturday morning, I woke up and made my way into the living room. To my surprise, she was already up and seated on the couch with a book in her hand. I had thought everyone would still be asleep. I sat down next to her on the couch and said, "What are you reading?"

"Oh, I was just scanning through your library, and this book caught my eye," she replied. "I had just read a few pages when you walked in."

She then closed the book and showed me the cover. The book was entitled *Eternal Security: How to Be Saved and Know It*. I'll never forget what she said next. "So, what does that mean to be saved and know it? How can you *truly* be saved and *know* it?"

This was it. I suddenly felt the presence of the Lord enter the room, and this was what he put on my heart to say: "Mom, when I was adopted into the Vaughan family, I became a Vaughan forever, and there's nothing that can change that. The Bible says that when the Lord saves us, He literally adopts us into the family of God, and there's nothing that we can do to change that."

I saw the Lord open her eyes right there in front of me. The scales had been removed, and the conviction began to set in. She began to cry and said, "You just make it sound so easy."

I replied, "Being saved is the easiest thing in the world to do. God has already done all of the work. He sent His only begotten Son, Jesus Christ, to pay for your sins with His own blood. He wrote the Word of God as a love letter to tell you about His sacrificial love, and He sent His Holy Spirit this morning to convict you and to convince you that it's true. All you have to do is give up."

At this point, I could tell that she didn't want to talk about it anymore. She wasn't angry or anything, but she looked scared to death. I decided it would be best if I just backed off. So that's what I did. I just told her that if she ever had any questions that I would be there. She thanked me as she got up to go to the restroom. I knew at that moment that it would just be a matter of time.

We went about our day and kept a certain level of normalcy, but it was obvious that she was dying inside. Her mind was just in another place, an eternal place. She would tear up periodically throughout the day. She seemed like someone who had just tragically lost a loved one and was in the first few days of the grieving process. Anyone who doesn't believe in Holy Ghost conviction never saw my birth mom. She is an extremely levelheaded and strong person, but that weekend she was a basket case.

The next day we all got up and went to church together. The Lord didn't even give her a break during Sunday school. "Coincidentally," Brother Ronnie just so happened to be teaching about the love of God for His children out of the book of 1 John. He even talked about how God adopts us into His family. I didn't want to stare at Mom, but I glanced over at her a couple of times, and I could see her crying heavily. Brother Ronnie casually walked over to her and handed her some tissues as he continued with the lesson. The Lord was putting her through the ringer of conviction.

When Sunday school was over and the room began to clear out, Brother Ronnie approached her and said, "Cheryl, is there anything you would like to talk to me about?" Mom threw her hands up in the air and said, "No!" She hurried out the door and into the hallway before he could say another word. Brother Ronnie and I looked at each other and grinned like a couple of Cheshire cats, because we both knew what the Lord was doing in her heart.

She cried during the morning service but didn't make a move. She cried off and on all afternoon, but she didn't say a word about what was wrong. She cried during the evening service, and still nothing happened. But after the evening service, Leah and I were on the stage, singing with one of our church members, when I noticed that Mom was seated on the front pew with Brother Ronnie. Normally we would have finished practicing, but we kept singing and singing. I didn't want to distract her at all. They talked for about ten minutes before I saw Mom and Mrs. Vickie, Brother Ronnie's wife, get up and head to the office over in the educational building.

As soon as they walked out the door, I stopped singing, looked at Brother Ronnie, and said, "Well?"

"We need to all gather around and pray for her. The Lord is really dealing with her about salvation," he said. So all of the church members who were still in the sanctuary gathered around, and we prayed for her.

Cheryl's Perspective

I couldn't help but feel a little crazy as I followed Vickie to the educational building. Ever since the day before, when I had talked with Brandon about salvation, something strange had been going on inside of me, something out of this world. For the first time in my life, I saw myself as someone lost and in need. I didn't fully understand what was going on, but I knew beyond a shadow of a doubt that it was real. It was wreaking havoc in my heart, and it was almost impossible to ignore. I at least wanted to talk to someone and try to find out what was happening.

By the time Vickie and I made it into Brother Ronnie's office, I was weeping almost uncontrollably. I sat down on the couch, while Vickie got some tissues off the desk. She handed them to me as she sat down beside me. After giving me a minute to calm down, she said in a soft voice, "I don't think that there is any way that this whole situation with Brandon is a coincidence, do you?"

"Absolutely not," I replied. That was one thing I was sure about.

Then Vickie cut right to the heart of the matter. "Do you know that you need to be saved from your sin?" I began to cry heavily again, but I nodded my head. "Yes." That was another thing that I was sure about at this point. But I also had some reservations about a few things.

I looked at Vickie and said, "But I just don't feel worthy. I've done some horrible things in my life."

Vickie compassionately replied, "Nobody is worthy of God's forgiveness, but He offers it to us anyway. I want to show you a verse of Scripture, if that's okay." I obliged. She then turned to Romans 10:13 and read, "For whosoever shall call upon the name of the Lord shall be saved." That word *whosoever* made me feel a lot better, because I knew that it included me. However, I still had some fears that needed to be dealt with.

I sat up on the edge of the couch and said, "I'm just so worried about how this will look if I get saved. I mean, people will think that I just did it for Brandon, and I'm worried that he will be criticized for it."

Vickie calmly replied, "I've known Brandon for a long time, and I can promise you that he doesn't care one bit about that. He would rather see his mom saved." I knew that she was absolutely right, but I was still scared and grasping at straws.

I made one last, feeble attempt at an excuse. "I know that I need to be saved, but I just feel like I need to get some things ironed out first."

Vickie replied, "If we wait until we have everything ironed out before we come to God, then we will *never* come to Him. You need to go to the Lord first, and He will iron everything out *for* you." She then began flipping through the pages of her Bible until she came to 2 Corinthians 6:2. "Behold, now is the accepted time; behold, now is the day of salvation," she read aloud. She then pointed her finger at the page and asked, "What does that word right there say?"

"*Now*," I replied. "Well then, there is your answer," she said. As I was teetering on the edge of eternity, Vickie made one final plea.

"Cheryl, do you believe that Jesus Christ was crucified for your sins and rose from the dead on the third day?"

"Yes, I believe that," I replied.

"Do you also believe that God orchestrated this whole ordeal with Brandon to bring you to Him?" she asked.

"There's not a doubt in my mind," I replied.

She said, "Then what are you waiting for?"

I knew that she was absolutely right. I was drowning in a sea of sin and guilt, and the Lord was throwing me a line. Someone who's drowning doesn't pass up a lifeline just because he hasn't had a chance to examine the boat that's pulling him to safety. He just grabs it and holds on tight. Without further hesitation, I bowed my head and cried out to God. I don't remember everything I said, but I do know that I asked Him to forgive me of my sins and to take my life and use it for His glory. Before I had even finished praying, I could feel the weight of the world lifted off my shoulders! It was as if there was new life inside of me. I felt so free, so clean! It was so real. This was what Brandon had been trying to tell me about.

As soon as I got through praying, Vickie began to pray, and she was crying heavily as well. After she got through praying, we spent the next few minutes laughing and crying together as we rejoiced over what the Lord had done. Suddenly she spoke up and said, "Let's go tell everyone!"

Brandon's Perspective

Mom had been with Mrs. Vickie for about twenty-five minutes or so, when they walked back into the sanctuary together. My mom had such a glow on her face. She didn't even have to tell me what had happened. I already knew. Mrs. Vicki said, "Cheryl has got something that she wants to tell everyone." Everybody looked at Mom as she spoke up and said, "I got saved!" My heart leaped for joy inside of me! It appeared that the Lord had brought everything full circle.

She walked up to me and gave me a bear hug. She looked at me and said, "You know that I didn't do this for you, right?"

"Mom, I wouldn't have let you do it just for me," I replied. "It was completely between you and God."

It was a joyous occasion. Everyone who was still in the sanctuary was rejoicing over all that the Lord had done. It really didn't seem real; it was like some kind of a dream. After we fellowshipped for a while, everyone began making their way to the door. We said our good-byes and headed back to Gordo.

July 29, 2012
Brandon's Perspective

There we were, my mom and I, wading into the baptistery at my church, dressed in white robes. What a special blessing this was going to be! It's not every day that someone gets the privilege of baptizing his birth mom after being reunited only five months before.

As we stood there in front of the Sunday morning crowd, I spoke up and said, "I'm so thankful to be standing here today with my birth mom. This is an absolute picture of the amazing grace of God! We were separated when I was born, but we were reconciled back in February. Even more importantly, she was reconciled to God through His Son, Jesus Christ, back in May. The Bible says that water baptism is a "like figure of the resurrection." It is an outward picture of an inward salvation that has taken place. Water baptism is like a wedding ring. The ring itself doesn't make a person married, but it shows the world that they *are*. My birth mom has been married to Jesus Christ, and it is my privilege this morning to be the ring bearer."

With all of that said, I looked at Mom and said, "Mom, do you know for sure that you're saved and on your way to heaven?"

Without any hesitation, she nodded her head and said, "Yes, I do."

With that, I put my left hand on her back, lifted my right hand into the air and said, "Then it's my privilege to baptize you, my sister, in the name of the Father, the Son, and the Holy Ghost."

Cheryl's Perspective

After those words, Brandon submerged me under the water. For those two seconds of weightless bliss, time seemed to come to a complete standstill. My mind went back one last time to that hospital delivery room in 1984. I was lying on my back in that bed with my eyes closed, giving birth to a son that I'd never thought I would get to see or hold or even know. Yet here I was again, lying on my back with my eyes closed—only this time that same son was holding *me*.

It's simply unspeakable, the things that God has done for us this year. I guess that's why they call it "Amazing Grace." I don't know what lies ahead on the path that God has chosen for Brandon and me. I have no doubt there will be mountaintops as well as valleys. But no matter what path God chooses for us to walk, this time we'll be able to walk it together.

18
Closing Thoughts

IF THERE IS ONE REGRET THAT I have about writing this book, it would be that the book has come to an end, while the story continues on. Just since August, when I began writing this book, God has given us so many added blessings. For starters, my birth mom joined a good church not far from her house. We have also had the opportunity to publicly share our testimonies from each of our perspectives.

This year has certainly been a year of firsts. Just a few weeks ago, we shared our first Thanksgiving together. Leah and the kids and I traveled to Florida for the holiday. This November was also the first time that Mom could celebrate my birthday with me and not have to worry about where I was. Even as I type these closing thoughts, we are only a couple of weeks away from celebrating our first Christmas together. The whole family is coming to Alabama.

We have no doubt that this is just the beginning of our story. Perhaps one day I'll get to write the sequel. My question to the reader is simply this: what about *your* story? God has a plan for your life. Hebrews 12:1 tells us that God has a specific race for everyone, and the hindrance to our running that race is the sin and the weight that we refuse to lay down.

Dear reader, who is holding the pen? Are you writing the story of your life, or have you truly given control to the Master. He's a lot better author than you and me, and He'll write a story that's a whole lot better than anyone could ever dream of.

Think about the heroes of the faith in Hebrews 11. Abel was a lowly shepherd, Moses was an orphan, and Rahab was even a harlot, just to name a few of those heroes. God saved them all and used them in mighty ways—not because they were special but because they were faithful in the little things, and God was able to do big things with their lives. God's not asking us to do anything big. He's just asking for some faithfulness, and He will do big things with our lives.

I just want to say in closing that there is nothing like living for the Lord! There is no greater satisfaction than doing the work that God has called *you* to do. In the eyes of the world, I am nothing. I don't make much money. I'm not the most athletic. I don't have much education. But I sure do have a story to tell! I give all the glory and praise to God and His amazing grace!

I'll leave the reader with an illustration given by the evangelist Dana Williams. Brother Dana preaches a sermon entitled "There Is Help in Egypt." In that sermon, he brings out the truth that God manifests Himself even in the evil world in which we live, and he uses a specific example concerning Moses' mother to prove his point.

The Israelites were multiplying at a rate that alarmed Pharaoh. He then enacted a decree that all Hebrew boys should be killed. So Moses' mother hid him for three months, until she couldn't hide him anymore. She then placed him in a basket and sent him down the Nile River. Moses' sister followed him from a distance to see what would become of him. Lo and behold, Pharaoh's daughter just so happened to be bathing in the river when Moses floated by. She had compassion for him and decided to adopt him.

Moses' sister spoke up and asked Pharaoh's daughter if she needed her to fetch a Hebrew midwife to nurse and care for the baby, and the princess obliged. Of course, Moses' sister went back to get her mother, and the rest was history. As Brother Dana so eloquently put it, "The last time that Moses' mother saw him, he was floating down the crocodile-infested Nile. The next time she saw him, he was in the arms of a government official who was asking if she would take care of this little baby boy. Then they offered to pay her to take care of her own son, and you know that Pharaoh didn't allow his grandson to live in a dump! I can see Moses' mother rocking him to sleep in the new house that Pharaoh had just built for them, and as she looked up at her husband, she said, 'You know, it wasn't supposed to be this good.'"

That's exactly how my mother and I feel when we think about our story. Never in a million years did we expect God to do something so amazing! It was the same way for Moses and his parents. No one could have expected it to be *that* good. God used Pharaoh to take care of the future redeemer of Israel! Moses' mother literally gave God the pen concerning the story of her son. She put him in a basket and sent him on his way. Dear reader, why don't you give the pen of your life to God and see what He does with it? Who knows? I might just get to read your story one day.

"But without faith it is impossible to please him; for he that cometh to God must believe that he is, and that he is a rewarder of them that diligently seek him" (Hebrews 11:6).

For more pictures, and to hear Brandon and Cheryl's testimonies, go to www.reconciled.weebly.com.

Appendix 1

How to Be Saved and Know It: The ABCs

Acknowledge **your need.**

Many people hear the word *saved* and ask themselves, "Saved from what?" The answer is simple: you need to be saved from your sin.

Romans 3:23 says, "For all have sinned and come short of the glory of God." We have all broken God's law and have fallen short of His perfect standard.

God in His holiness must punish sin: "For the wages of sin is death" (Romans 6:23a). That death is an eternity in the lake of fire: "And whosoever was not found written in the book of life was cast into the lake of fire" (Revelation 20:15).

You need to be saved from the penalty and power of your sin!

Believe **on the Lord Jesus Christ.**

God in His holiness must punish sin, but God in His love sent His Son, Jesus Christ, to shoulder the punishment for us. "For he hath made him to be sin for us, who knew no sin; that we might be made the righteousness of God in him" (2 Corinthians 5:21).

"For God so loved the world that he gave his only begotten Son, that whosoever believeth in him should not perish but have everlasting life" (John 3:16). This belief is not a simple head knowledge but a life-changing heart knowledge. "For godly sorrow worketh repentance to salvation not to be repented of: but the sorrow of the world worketh death" (2 Corinthians 7:10). "Therefore if any man be in Christ, he is a new creature: old things are passed away; behold, all things are become new" (2 Corinthians 5:17).

Call **upon the name of the Lord.**

He has never turned anyone away. He will take you as you are, but He won't leave you the same! "For whosoever shall call upon the name of the Lord shall be saved" (Romans 10:13). "That if thou shalt confess with thy mouth the Lord Jesus, and shalt believe in thine heart that God hath raised him from the dead, thou shalt be saved. For with the heart man believeth unto righteousness; and with the mouth confession is made unto salvation" (Romans 10:9–10).

What are you waiting for, my friend? Repent and call upon the name of the Lord to save you. He will be the best thing that ever happened to you!

Appendix 2

Adoption 101

L ET ME START BY SAYING THAT I don't claim to be any kind of expert when it comes to life-changing decisions for your family. I just wanted to give some basic advice that comes from my experience as an adoptee, which may be a help to some. The following subjects deal with some common questions that I have been asked in the past few years. Please feel free to take my advice with a grain of salt.

Looking to Adopt

Ever since I was adopted, the agency has sent us a quarterly newsletter. The last one we got in the mail contained an astonishing statistic. It said that three out of five people in America are somehow affected by adoption. Chances are, if you're taking time to read this appendix, that you have been unsuccessful in your attempt to conceive children. Almost without exception, it is the dream of every married couple to conceive children of their own. However, many times life happens while we're busy making plans.

But I have good news for the Christian married couple that cannot conceive on their own. God is in control! The Bible makes it clear that it is the Lord who opens and shuts the womb. Genesis 20:18 says, "For the Lord had fast closed up all the wombs of the house of Abimelech." Also, in chapter one of 1 Samuel, we find that God opened the womb of Hannah, and she was able to conceive Samuel.

It's a significant comfort to know that it's not simply a medical matter but one of divine cause. I can tell you with confidence that God has a child out there just for you, although it may not come from you. My mom miscarried twin boys before she finally started to look into adoption, and that was how they got me. If all of the good Christian people in the world could have children of their own, what would become of all of the orphans? Perhaps you should prayerfully consider adoption.

Telling Children That They Are Adopted

I am of the firm opinion that the younger children are when they learn that they are adopted, the better. And honesty is the best policy. My parents told me the truth about my adoption when I was about five years old. The timing was good, because I was old enough to understand it, but I *wasn't* old enough to internalize it too much. Because I grew up knowing that I was adopted, I never felt later like I had lived a lie. If my adoptive parents had waited until I was a good bit older, I might have felt like I had been living a lie in thinking that they were my birth parents.

If you feel that perhaps you would like to wait until your child is a little older than I was, I highly recommend telling them before the teenage years. Adolescence is a huge transition period for anyone. Throw in an "Oh, by the way" concerning their adoption, and it could be a mess.

Adoptees Looking for Birth Parents

Let me begin by saying that you ultimately need to seek the Lord and see what *He* wants you to do. If I had listened to everyone else, I *never* would have searched for my birth mom. That being said, let me warn you that, for the overwhelming majority of adoptees, it's not a happy ending like it was for me. I feel very blessed and fortunate that it worked out the way it did. I could fill up a whole chapter with all of the horror stories I've heard about adoptees being completely and utterly rejected by their birth parents. Personally, I think it's a guilt thing, but I'm really not sure.

If you *do* decide to go through with it and look for your birth parents, there are some things that may be of help to you.

First of all, you need to set some realistic goals and expectations. You need to ask yourself why you want to find them and what you expect out of the relationship, should you succeed. Personally, I had made up my mind that even if my birth mom wanted nothing to do with me, I wanted her to know that I was okay and that I had no hard feelings. I also wanted to share the gospel with her. The old saying, "Expect the worst and hope for the best," is an accurate way to describe the approach to your search, because the truth is that if you *are* rejected, it *will* hurt.

One of the best tips that I can give on the actual search process would be to start close and work your way out. In other words, talk to your parents or someone who knows about the details of the adoption and go from there. If you can't find your birth parents on your own, your absolute best bet is a private investigator. They are relatively inexpensive and highly effective. If it hadn't been for Florida's insanely strict privacy laws, a private investigator could have helped me.

Be very careful about so-called reunion companies. I had one group wanting to charge me thirteen hundred dollars. They told me it could take up to two years, and there were *no guarantees*. Also, if you do happen to locate your birth parents, please remember to *use a mediator* the first time you contact them. It will save them the heart attack and soften the blow of rejection for you, should that be the case. Your mediator should be someone you can trust. My wife Leah did an excellent job for me.

I hope this has been a help to you. God bless you in your search.

Appendix 3

Pregnant and Scared

D EAR HEART, IF THIS APPENDIX CAUGHT your eye because you are in this situation, I want to encourage you. No matter what's in your past, God will forgive you, and no matter what's in your future, God will take care of you. My birth mom was pregnant and scared at one point in her life too. At that time in her life, taking care of a child seemed like the furthest thing from possible. However, she did the right thing even though it was hard.

I'm writing this appendix to try and help you. The worst thing that could happen is for one giant mistake to turn into *two* giant mistakes. Abortion is a multimillion-dollar industry. Abortion groups try to pressure scared and vulnerable girls like my birth mom into having an abortion. They make it sound like it's best for the child if it is never born, given the circumstances it would be born into. But this is nothing but a "mercy killing." These organizations care nothing about you or your child. I'm so glad that my mom didn't go that route.

The Bible makes it clear in Jeremiah 1:5—as well as several other passages—that it's not just fetus in the womb. It is a child! Abortion stops a beating heart. You may not even be a Bible-believer, but one thing that no one can argue with is that abortion destroys a potential human life, a potential father or mother, a potential doctor or nurse—and, yes, even a potential preacher. God has a plan for your child!

The truth is that abortion isn't an easy way out, because you will just be trading fear for overwhelming guilt. Make no mistake about it: abortion doesn't make you un-pregnant; it makes you the parent of a dead child. If you're pregnant and have no way of caring for a child, perhaps you should prayerfully consider adoption. As in our case, you never know how the Lord might bring that child back to you. There are many more options for adoption today than there were in the eighties. For example, open adoption is now a common practice. This would save mothers from experiencing much of the pain and worry that my mother had to deal with as a result of my closed adoption.

Perhaps you are reading this and have already been through an abortion. I'm not here to judge you; I want to help you. If you have had an abortion, I can give you two promises from the Word of God. First of all, your baby is in heaven with the Lord (2 Samuel 12:18–23). Secondly, the Lord will forgive you and take away your guilt. "If we confess our sins, he is faithful and just to forgive us our sins, and to cleanse us from all unrighteousness" (1 John 1:9).

Whatever place you find yourself in right now, the Lord loves you, and He is able! Just trust Him and see what He can do with your situation.